FEMA Incident Management and Support Keystone

January 2011

U.S. Department of Homeland Security
500 C Street, SW
Washington, DC 20472

JAN 12 2011

FEMA

MEMORANDUM FOR: All FEMA Employees

FROM: William L. Carwile, III
          Associate Administrator for Response and Recovery

SUBJECT: Incident Management and Support Keystone

In the Administrator's December 11, 2009 memorandum, *FEMA Strategic Focus for 2010*, he identified three strategic objectives as key areas of focus for FEMA for 2010. One is doctrine development and implementation. In support of this objective we have completed the development of capstone, *FEMA Publication 1* which reflects organizational purpose, history, values, and guiding principles for FEMA. In addition, the Office of Response and Recovery and a team of disaster experts have developed the fundamental incident management and support doctrine for FEMA.

With this memorandum, I am providing FEMA's *Incident Management and Support Keystone*. This document describes key tenets and concepts for managing operations. It is an important foundational support element of the Agency's new overarching *FEMA Publication 1*. It also provides a renewed commitment to the National Response Framework, the principles of disaster recovery, the National Incident Management System, and will provide a foundation for our continued effort to empower the Regions and emergency managers in the field.

As written, this doctrine thoroughly addresses the functions of response, recovery, logistics and mitigation during incident management and incident support operations. I ask that all FEMA staff, as emergency managers, review the *Incident Management and Support Keystone*. Its release is a major step forward in building our comprehensive library of agency doctrine. Because this document will help guide doctrine and procedure development in the future, I ask that you fully support the implementation of its concepts.

If you have any questions regarding this publication please contact the Training, Exercise and Doctrine Office at FEMA-TED@fema.gov.

Attachments: *Incident Management and Support Keystone*

CONTENTS

Contents 4

Chapter 1: Introduction 1

Purpose 1
Scope2
Foundational Documents and Authorities...............................3
Background 5

Chapter 2: National Response Framework Doctrine......................6

1. Engaged Partnership...6
2. Tiered Response..6
3. Scalable, Flexible, and Adaptable Operational Capabilities 7
4. Unity of Effort Through Unified Command.........................7
5. Readiness to Act...8

Chapter 3: Recovery Core Principles 9

1. Individual and Family Empowerment 9
2. Leadership and Local Primacy...9
3. Pre-disaster Planning..10
4. Partnerships and Inclusiveness 10
5. Public Information...10
6. Unity of Effort..11
7. Timeliness and Flexibility 11
8. Resilience and Sustainability..11
9. Psychological and Emotional Recovery 11

Chapter 4: FEMA's Incident Management and Support Tenets.........12

Tenet 1: Engage the Whole Community 12
Tenet 2: Empower Emergency Managers to Make Decisions and Take
    Coordinated Action..14
Tenet 3: Respond Quickly With Decisive Initial Actions................15
Tenet 4: Use Outcome-Based Objectives..............................16
Tenet 5: Develop Creative Solutions and Atypical Resources.........17

Chapter 5: FEMA Incident Management and Support Key Concepts 19

Concept 1: Incident Management and Support Are Conducted in Accordance With NIMS 20

Concept 2: Effective Preparedness Provides the Basis for Successful Incident Management and Support 26

Concept 3: Incidents Are Categorized by Disaster Levels to Guide Deployment of Resources 27

Concept 4: Incidents Should Be Managed at the Lowest Possible Operational Level 28

Concept 5: Unity of Effort in Response Is Achieved Through Unified Command. Unity of Effort in Recovery is Achieved Through Unity of Purpose 29

Concept 6: Disciplined Priorities Enable Meaningful Objectives 31

Concept 7: Establishing a Secure Operating Environment, Including Emergency Routes, Is Essential to Effective Incident Management and Support 31

Concept 8: Disaster Emergency Communications Are Essential to Effective Incident Management and Support 32

Concept 9: Anticipate Potential Requirements and Quickly Move Resources to Support the Response and Short-Term Recovery 32

Concept 10: Enable Citizens and Survivors to Assist Their Communities Before, During, and After an Incident 33

Concept 11: Response and Recovery Actions Must Be Targeted to Assist the Most Vulnerable 34

Concept 12: Response, Recovery, and Mitigation Activities Operate Concurrently as Part of Incident Management and Support 34

Concept 13: Response and Recovery decisions are informed by risk analysis 35

Concept 14: Planning Is the Foundation for Achieving Common Objectives Through Integrated Response and Recovery Efforts 35

Concept 15: Successful Incident Management and Support Is Ultimately Accomplished When Communities Are More Resilient and Sustainable than They Were Before the Incident 36

Concept 16: Incident Planning Is a Key Activity at All Echelons of FEMA Response and Recovery 37

Concept 17: There Is Only One Incident Action Plan (IAP) for Each Incident, and the IAP Is Developed Only at the Incident Level 41

Concept 18: Effective Incident Planning Requires a Comprehensive System for Information Collection, Sharing, and Analysis That Includes All Echelons of an Incident 41

Concept 19: Deliberate Planning is the Foundation for Incident Planning 43

Concept 20: Deliberate Planning Is Only as Effective as Its Ability to Guide Actual Operations 43

Chapter 6: Applying FEMA Incident Management and Support Doctrine 45

Key Roles and Responsibilities 45

FEMA's Incident Command and Management Organization 51

Conclusion...53

CHAPTER 1: INTRODUCTION

PURPOSE

This Federal Emergency Management Agency (FEMA) Incident Management and Support Keystone establishes the foundational doctrine that guides FEMA's conduct of disaster operations.

This Keystone is the primary document from which all other FEMA disaster response, recovery, mitigation, and logistics directives and policies are derived. It describes how the response doctrine, articulated in the National Response Framework (NRF), and recovery doctrine are implemented in the context of FEMA incident management and support operations. This Keystone is fully in line with the National Incident Management System.

> **FEMA's mission is to support U.S. citizens and first responders to ensure that, as a nation, we work together to build, sustain, and improve our capability to prepare for, protect against, respond to, recover from, and mitigate all hazards.**

Incident Management is the incident-level operation of the Federal role in emergency response, recovery, logistics, and mitigation. Responsibilities in incident management include the direct control and employment of resources, management of incident offices, operations, and delivery of Federal assistance through all phases of emergency response.

Incident Support is the coordination of all Federal resources that support emergency response, recovery, logistics, and mitigation. Responsibilities include the deployment of national-level assets, support of national objectives and programs affected during the disaster, and support of incident operations with resources, expertise, information, and guidance.

This keystone document describes the full function of FEMA assistance, from the earliest lifesaving operations and support through the entire life of the Joint Field Office (JFO). The keystone addresses how FEMA will provide lifesaving operations and necessary resources; restore power and rebuild roads in the affected communities; provide technical assistance to community floodplain management programs and flood insurance; and manage individual assistance inspections, temporary housing, public assistance inspections, 406 mitigation, and hazard mitigation grants. The Incident Management and Support Keystone leads a family of other doctrinal documents that guide the implementation of FEMA's disaster operations. This document is intended to

- standardize procedures,
- institutionalize best practices, and
- guide planning, training, equipping, and staffing.

Doctrine is an authoritative statement of fundamental principles of an organization. It is authoritative yet—when applied with judgment—adaptable enough to address diverse situations. Doctrine provides a standard frame of reference for FEMA and explains why the Agency performs its functions. Doctrine is a guide to action and judgment founded in hard-won experience; it facilitates readiness and increased efficiency and effectiveness by standardizing activities and processes. Doctrine links theory, experience, innovation, and practice.

Doctrine shows how the key actors in an incident align their processes to promote coordinated and effective outcomes. It provides a basis for enhanced capabilities through training, staffing, equipping, exercises, and future concept development. It directly influences how policy and plans are developed and implemented, how FEMA organizes to achieve its mission, and how resource requirement decisions are made. The consistent application of doctrine outlined in this Keystone will assist FEMA in better managing its functions, requirements, capabilities, priorities, policies, organizational design, command and control authorities, and the allocation of resources across the full spectrum of disaster response and recovery.

> **Incident:** An occurrence, natural or man-made, that requires a response to protect life or property. Incidents can, for example, include major disasters, emergencies, terrorist attacks, terrorist threats, civil unrest, wildland and urban fires, floods, hazardous material spills, nuclear accidents, aircraft accidents, earthquakes, hurricanes, tornadoes, tropical storms, tsunamis, war-related disasters, public health and medical emergencies, and other occurrences requiring response and recovery efforts.
>
> (Source: National Incident Management System)

SCOPE

This FEMA Incident Management and Support Keystone applies to all FEMA incident management and support operations, including incidents that have occurred, efforts undertaken based on an identified threat, and actions performed in anticipation of, or in preparation for, a significant event.

This doctrine pertains to FEMA incident management and support operations that involve— or that *may* involve—a presidential declaration under the Stafford Act, as well as incidents requiring a coordinated Federal response where the Stafford Act does not apply. This doctrine applies to the full range of incidents contained within one or several jurisdictions, as well as those incidents that are national in scope.

This Keystone is intended to promote readiness to act, effective cooperation, interoperability, and sharing of essential resources and information among all levels of government, nongovernmental organizations (NGOs), and the private sector—by communicating to our partners the principles by which FEMA conducts incident management and support operations.

FOUNDATIONAL DOCUMENTS AND AUTHORITIES

A number of foundational documents provide statutory, regulatory, and executive guidance for FEMA disaster response. Some key foundational documents are as follows:

- *Robert T. Stafford Disaster Relief and Emergency Assistance Act (Public Law 93-288, as amended, 42 U.S.C. 5121-5207).* The Stafford Act authorizes the programs and processes by which the Federal Government provides disaster and emergency assistance to State and local governments, tribal nations, eligible private nonprofit organizations, and individuals affected by a declared major disaster or emergency. The Stafford Act covers all hazards, including natural disasters and terrorist events.

- *Title 44 of the Code of Federal Regulations (CFR), Emergency Management and Assistance.* The Code of Federal Regulations is a codification of the general and permanent rules and regulations published in the *Federal Register* that contain basic policies and procedures. Title 44 is entitled *Emergency Management and Assistance*, and Chapter 1 of Title 44 contains the regulations issued by FEMA, including those related to implementing the Stafford Act.

- *Homeland Security Act (Public Law 107-296, as amended, 6 U.S.C. §§ 101 et seq.).* The Homeland Security Act of 2002 created the Department of Homeland Security (DHS) as an executive department of the United States. The Homeland Security Act consolidated component agencies, including FEMA, into the Department. The Secretary of Homeland Security is the head of the Department and has direction, authority, and control over it. All functions of all officers, employees, and organizational units of the Department are vested in the Secretary. The mission of the Department includes preventing terrorist attacks within the United States, reducing America's vulnerability to terrorism, and minimizing the damage and recovering from attacks that occur. The Post-Katrina Emergency Management Reform Act of 2006 (described below) amended the Homeland Security Act with respect to the organizational structure, authorities, and responsibilities of FEMA and the FEMA Administrator.

- *Homeland Security Presidential Directive 5 (HSPD-5), 2003.* Homeland Security Presidential Directive 5 enhances the ability of the United States to manage domestic incidents by directing the establishment of a single, comprehensive National Incident Management System (NIMS). This management system is designed to cover the prevention of, preparation for, response to, and recovery from terrorist attacks, major disasters, and other emergencies. The system allows all levels of government throughout the Nation to work together efficiently and effectively. The directive gives further detail on which government officials oversee and have authority for various parts of the NIMS, and it makes several amendments to various other Homeland Security Presidential Directives.

- *Post-Katrina Emergency Management Reform Act of 2006 (Public Law 109-295), October 4, 2006.* The Post-Katrina Emergency Management Reform Act (PKEMRA) clarified and modified the Homeland Security Act with respect to the organizational structure, authorities, and responsibilities of FEMA and the FEMA Administrator. This act enhanced FEMA's responsibilities and its autonomy within DHS. Per PKEMRA, FEMA is to lead and support the Nation in a risk-based, comprehensive emergency management system of preparedness, protection, response, recovery, and mitigation. Under the act, the FEMA Administrator reports directly to the Secretary of Homeland Security. FEMA is now a distinct entity within DHS, and the Secretary of Homeland Security can no longer substantially or significantly reduce the authorities, responsibilities, or functions of FEMA—or the capability to perform them—unless authorized by subsequent legislation. The act further directed the transfer to FEMA of many of the functions of DHS's former Preparedness Directorate.

- *National Response Framework (NRF), January 2008.* The NRF is a guide to how the Nation conducts all-hazards response. It is built upon scalable, flexible, and adaptable coordinating structures to align key roles and responsibilities across the Nation, linking all levels of government, NGOs, and the private sector. The NRF is intended to capture specific authorities and best practices for managing incidents that range from serious but purely local events, to large-scale terrorist attacks or catastrophic natural disasters.[1]

- *National Incident Management System (NIMS), December 2008.* The NIMS is a set of principles that provides a systematic, proactive approach to guiding government agencies at all levels, NGOs, and the private sector to work seamlessly to prevent, protect against, respond to, recover from, and mitigate the effects of incidents—regardless of cause, size, location, or complexity—in order to reduce the loss of life or property and harm to the environment.

---

[1] Catastrophic incident: An incident of such magnitude that all available assets that were designed and put in place for response are completely overwhelmed or broken at the incident, regional, or national level.

Background

Over the past 30 years, FEMA has been called upon repeatedly to become engaged not only to deliver the traditional recovery programs but also to coordinate the delivery of emergency services—services such as search and rescue, emergency power, debris clearance, emergency communications, emergency roofing, disaster housing, and other commodities to support State, local, tribal and Federal incident response operations.

The failure to provide these services in a timely and coordinated manner with Federal, State, local and tribal partners resulted in the criticism that FEMA received following incidents such as Hurricane Hugo (1989), Hurricane Andrew (1992), and Hurricane Katrina (2005). In response to these experiences, FEMA altered its focus and organization in fundamental ways. During the 1990s, the organization reduced its emphasis on civil defense and prioritized the natural disaster response system. FEMA gave greater attention to mitigation and preparedness as well. Following these efforts, FEMA's scope and responsibility increased in the mid-2000s through executive and legislative action.

As the Nation's professional emergency management organization, FEMA continues to make a concerted effort to build, sustain, and improve its ability to assist State and local governments by developing and using standards and doctrine to expedite the delivery of these emergency services. While statutes and executive orders give FEMA the authority to act, doctrine explains *why* and *how* Federal emergency managers act as they do.

Chapter 2: National Response Framework Doctrine

The National Response Framework (NRF) is the definitive authority for national response in the United States. It guides how our Nation responds to all hazards. The framework therefore provides the basis for all FEMA response doctrine.

The NRF defines basic roles, responsibilities, and operational concepts for response across all levels of government, with nongovernmental organizations (NGOs), and with the private sector. The overarching objective of response activities centers on saving lives and protecting property and the environment.

The key principles articulated in the NRF Response Doctrine are of such significance to this response operations keystone that they are included here. According to the NRF, these principles are rooted in America's Federal system and the Constitution's division of responsibilities between Federal and State governments.

> **NRF Response Doctrine— Key Principles**
>
> 1. Engaged partnership
> 2. Tiered response
> 3. Scalable, flexible, and adaptable operational capabilities
> 4. Unity of effort through unified command
> 5. Readiness to act

1. Engaged Partnership

Leaders at all levels must communicate and actively support partnerships by developing shared goals and aligning capabilities so that no one is overwhelmed in times of crisis. Layered, mutually-supporting capabilities at Federal, State, tribal, and local levels allow for planning together in times of calm and responding together effectively in times of need. Engaged partnership includes ongoing communication of incident activity among all partners and shared situational awareness for a more rapid response.

Engaged partnerships are essential to preparedness. Effective response begins with a host of preparedness activities conducted well in advance of an incident. Preparedness involves a combination of planning, resources, training, exercising, and organizing to build, sustain, and improve operational capabilities. Preparedness is the process of identifying the personnel, training, and equipment needed for a wide range of potential incidents and developing jurisdiction-specific plans for delivering capabilities when needed for an incident.

2. Tiered Response

Incidents must be managed at the lowest possible jurisdictional level and supported by additional capabilities when needed. Each level need not be overwhelmed prior to requesting resources from another level.

Incidents begin and end locally, and most are wholly managed at the local level. Many incidents require unified response from local agencies, NGOs, and the private sector, and some require additional support from neighboring jurisdictions or the particular State involved. A small number require Federal support. National response protocols recognize this and are structured to provide additional tiered levels of support when there is a need for more resources or capabilities to support and sustain the response and initial recovery. All levels should be prepared to respond, anticipating resources that may be required.

3. SCALABLE, FLEXIBLE, AND ADAPTABLE OPERATIONAL CAPABILITIES

As incidents change in size, scope, and complexity, the response must adapt to meet requirements. The number, type, and sources of resources must be able to expand rapidly to meet needs associated with a given incident. The disciplined and coordinated process described in the NRF can provide for a rapid surge of resources from all levels of government, appropriately scaled to need. Execution must be flexible and adapted to fit each individual incident. Responders must also remain nimble and adaptable for the duration of a response, especially as needs grow and change. Equally, the overall response should be flexible as it transitions from the response effort to recovery.

4. UNITY OF EFFORT THROUGH UNIFIED COMMAND

Effective *unified command* is indispensable to response activities and requires a clear understanding of the roles and responsibilities of each participating organization. Success requires *unity of effort*, which respects the chain of command of each participating organization while harnessing seamless coordination across jurisdictions in support of common objectives.

The Incident Command System (ICS) and Multiagency Coordination System (MACS) are important elements across multijurisdictional or multiagency incident management activities. They provide structure to enable agencies with different legal, jurisdictional, and functional responsibilities to coordinate, plan, and interact effectively on scene. As a team effort, unified command allows all agencies with jurisdictional authority and/or functional responsibility for the incident to provide joint support through mutually developed incident objectives and strategies established at the command level. Each participating agency maintains its own authority, responsibility, and accountability.

The National Incident Management System (NIMS) supports response through the following elements of unified command: (1) developing a single set of objectives; (2) using a collective, strategic approach; (3) improving information flow and coordination; (4) creating a common understanding of joint priorities and restrictions; (5) ensuring that no agency's legal authorities are compromised or neglected; and (6) optimizing the combined efforts of all agencies under a single plan.

5. READINESS TO ACT

Effective response requires readiness to act balanced with an understanding of risk. From individuals, households, and communities to local, tribal, State, and Federal governments, national response depends on the instinct and ability to act. A forward-leaning posture is imperative both for incidents that could expand rapidly in size, scope, or complexity, and for no-notice incidents.

Once response activities have begun, on-scene actions are based on NIMS principles. To save lives and protect property and the environment, decisive on-scene action is often required of responders. Although some risk may be unavoidable, first responders anticipate and manage risk through proper training and planning.

Command—either single or unified—is responsible for establishing immediate priorities for the safety of not only the public, but also the responders and other emergency workers involved in the response, and for ensuring that adequate health and safety measures are in place.

Acting swiftly and effectively requires clear, focused communication and the processes to support it. Without effective communication, a bias toward action will be ineffectual at best, and likely perilous. An effective national response relies on disciplined processes, procedures, and systems to communicate timely, accurate, and accessible information on the incident's cause, size, and current situation to the public, responders, and others. Well-developed public information, education strategies, and communication plans help to ensure that lifesaving measures, evacuation routes, threat and alert systems, and other public safety information are coordinated and communicated to numerous diverse audiences in a consistent, accessible, and timely manner.

CHAPTER 3: RECOVERY CORE PRINCIPLES

The core principles and organizational constructs introduced coexist with the National Response Framework (NRF) and build upon its organizational structure and resources to more effectively address long-term recovery needs. The principles articulated in this chapter guide the full spectrum of recovery efforts with the recognition that recovery is a continuum. Recovery begins with pre-disaster preparedness and includes a broad spectrum of planning activities. That clarifies the roles and responsibilities for stakeholders in both pre- and post-disaster recovery efforts. It also recognizes that disaster, when it occurs, impacts some segments of the population more than others.

1. INDIVIDUAL AND FAMILY EMPOWERMENT

All community members must have equal opportunity to participate in community recovery efforts in a meaningful way. Care must be taken to assure that actions, both intentional and unintentional, do not exclude groups of people based on race, color, national origin (including limited English proficiency), religion, sex or disability. Care must be taken to identify and eradicate social and institutional barriers that hinder or preclude individuals with disabilities and others in the community historically subjected to unequal treatment from full and equal enjoyment of the programs, goods, services, activities, facilities, privileges, advantages, and accommodations provided. A successful recovery is about the ability of individuals and families to rebound from their losses in a manner that sustains their physical, emotional, social and economic well-being. The restoration of infrastructure systems and services is critical during recovery. It is vital that all individuals who make up the community are provided with the tools to access and use a continuum of care that addresses both the physical losses sustained and the psychological and emotional trauma experienced.

2. LEADERSHIP AND LOCAL PRIMACY

Successful recovery requires informed and coordinated leadership throughout all levels of government, sectors of society and phases of the recovery process. It recognizes that local, state and tribal governments have primary responsibility for the recovery of their communities and play the lead role in planning for and managing all aspects of community recovery. This is a basic, underlying principle that should not be overlooked by state, federal and other disaster recovery managers. States act in support of their communities, evaluate their capabilities and provide a means of support for overwhelmed local governments. The federal government is a partner and facilitator in recovery, prepared to enlarge its role when the disaster impacts relate to areas where federal jurisdiction is primary or affects national security. The federal government, while acknowledging the primary role of local, state and tribal governments, is prepared to vigorously support local, state and tribal governments in a large-scale or catastrophic incident.

3. Pre-disaster Planning

The speed and success of recovery can be greatly enhanced by advanced establishment of the process and protocols prior to a disaster for coordinated post-disaster recovery planning and implementation. All stakeholders should be involved to ensure a coordinated and comprehensive planning process, and develop relationships that increase post-disaster collaboration and unified decision-making. Another important objective of pre-disaster recovery planning is to take actions that will significantly reduce any disaster impacts that may occur by rebuilding a more disaster resistant and resilient community. Hence, the NDRF strongly encourages innovation among the states, localities, and the private sector in working together to identify state and locally-generated tools and resources, pre-disaster, that will serve to support and sustain disaster mitigation and long-term recovery efforts.

4. Partnerships and Inclusiveness

Partnerships and collaboration across groups, sectors and governments promote a successful recovery process. Partnerships and inclusiveness are vital for ensuring that all voices are heard from all parties involved in disaster recovery and that all available resources are brought to the table. This is especially critical at the community level where nongovernmental partners in the private and nonprofit sectors play a critical role in meeting local needs. Inclusiveness in the recovery process includes individuals with disabilities and others with access and functional needs, advocates of children, seniors and members of underserved communities. Sensitivity and respect for social and cultural diversity must be maintained at all times. Compliance with equal opportunity and civil rights laws must also be upheld.

5. Public Information

Clear, consistent, culturally appropriate and frequent communication initiatives promote successful public information outcomes. These incorporate a process that is inclusive and ensures accessibility to all, including those with disabilities, persons who are deaf or blind and those with limited English proficiency. Public information messaging helps manage expectations throughout the recovery process and supports the development of local, state and tribal government communications plans. This ensures stakeholders have a clear understanding of available assistance and their roles and responsibilities; makes clear the actual pace, requirements and time needed to achieve recovery; and includes information and referral help lines and websites for recovery resources.

6. Unity of Effort

A successful recovery process requires unity of effort, which respects the authority and expertise of each participating organization while coordinating support of common recovery objectives. Common objectives are built upon consensus and a transparent and inclusive planning process with clear metrics to measure progress.

7. Timeliness and Flexibility

A successful recovery process upholds the value of timeliness and flexibility in coordinating and efficiently conducting recovery activities and delivering assistance. It also minimizes delays and loss of opportunities. The process strategically sequences recovery decisions and promotes coordination; addresses potential conflicts; builds confidence and ownership of the recovery process among all stakeholders; and ensures recovery plans, programs, policies and practices are adaptable to meet unforeseen, unmet and evolving recovery needs.

8. Resilience and Sustainability

A successful recovery process promotes practices that minimize the community's risk to all hazards and strengthens its ability to withstand and recover from future disasters, which constitutes a community's resiliency. A successful recovery process engages in a rigorous assessment and understanding of risks and vulnerabilities that might endanger the community or pose additional recovery challenges. The process promotes implementation of the National Infrastructure Protection Plan (N I P P) risk management framework to enhance the resilience and protection of critical infrastructure against the effects of future disasters. Resilience incorporates hazard mitigation strategies; critical infrastructure, environmental and cultural resource protection; and sustainability practices not only in reconstructing the built environment, such as housing and infrastructure, but also in revitalizing the economic, social and natural environments.

9. Psychological and Emotional Recovery

A successful recovery process addresses the full range of psychological and emotional needs of the community as it recovers from the disaster through the provision of support, counseling, screening and treatment when needed. These needs range from helping individuals to handle the shock and stress associated with the disaster's impact and recovery challenges, to addressing the potential and consequences of individuals harming themselves or others through substance, physical and emotional abuses resulting from the disaster. Successful recovery acknowledges the linkages between the recovery of individuals, families and communities.

CHAPTER 4: FEMA's INCIDENT MANAGEMENT AND SUPPORT TENETS

Tenets are the core beliefs that FEMA emergency managers hold to be true. Tenets describe the core basis for action during response and recovery. They are consistent with and expand on the key principles articulated in the National Response Framework (NRF)—which apply to the Nation as a whole—by focusing on FEMA's role as a partner and provider. Tenets clearly guide the approach to any incident, regardless of size. These are enduring principles that frame the overall approach to conducting successful incident management and support

> **FEMA Incident Management and Support Tenets**
>
> 1. Engage the whole community.
> 2. Empower emergency managers to make decisions and take coordinated action.
> 3. Respond quickly with decisive initial actions.
> 4. Use outcome-based objectives.
> 5. Develop creative solutions and atypical resources.

operations and should be applied in virtually all circumstances. FEMA's tenets are the principles that a Federal emergency manager can fall back on to guide his or her actions during any situation. By adhering to these tenets, the manager can better conduct response and recovery operations. These tenets are a step forward, providing clear imperatives for bold, coordinated action when providing support.

TENET 1: ENGAGE THE WHOLE COMMUNITY

Responding to emergencies, especially major disasters, involves multiple agencies, organizations, and individuals. Locally, successful response and recovery require the combined efforts of the whole community, including local and tribal governments, nonprofits, faith-based organizations, other nongovernmental organizations (NGOs), private businesses, and individuals.

Recovering successfully from a disaster depends upon the interaction of a wide range of public and private programs and initiatives, including good planning, local capacity, effective leadership and decision-making structures, and public confidence-building. Recovery will engage members of a community who are neither first responders nor emergency personnel, creating significant challenges for coordinating and managing effective response and recovery.

The same principle applies at the Federal level. The power of the Federal Government's ability to assist State, local and tribal governments comes from combining the unique capabilities of all Federal departments and agencies—as well as the national private sector and NGOs— and bringing all of these capabilities to bear on the problem in a coordinated manner.

When an incident occurs that requires a Federal response, FEMA has two important roles:

1. FEMA applies its own resources. The following are examples:

    - Incident Management Assistance Teams (IMATs), search and rescue teams, and Preliminary Damage Assessment (PDA) teams

    - Caches of emergency commodities

    - Response, recovery, and mitigation personnel

2. FEMA marshals and coordinates the entire Federal government's response and recovery as follows:

    - National-, regional-, and incident-level incident management and support, such as the following:

        o Initial lifesaving/life-sustaining activities

        o Recovery and community support

        o Mitigation Assistance

    - Coordination and administration of statutory FEMA programs and assistance, such as the following:

        o Public Assistance

        o Individual Assistance

        o National Flood Insurance Program

Most Federal departments and agencies have unique capabilities, expertise, and relationships with public- and private-sector elements that are critically important to incident

> **Whole Community**
>
> The term *whole community*—with regard to disaster resilience— refers to the sum of the people and the commercial, economic, governmental, infrastructure, and social systems that make up a jurisdiction.

response efforts. In some cases Federal departments and agencies respond to incidents under their own statutory or executive authorities, rather than at FEMA's request. When this happens, the activities of those Federal departments and agencies must ultimately be integrated into the overall Federal response and support process.

During incident response operations, FEMA also works to enable the private sector to provide goods and services to the community. The most effective way to care for survivors is to reestablish the systems (stores, utilities, health care) that survivors need to care for themselves. The private sector provides most of these systems before an incident and will ultimately provide them again. When the private sector is operational, the community recovers more quickly by retaining jobs and a stable tax base. Accelerating the process of getting these private-sector elements back in business is a key emergency response priority. Assisting in this process is the American entrepreneurial spirit, which is an important asset in times of adversity. People want to help, and survivors themselves represent an important pool of support and expertise.

In catastrophes, engaging all normal emergency response and recovery resources is important, but it will not be enough. FEMA must work with Federal, State, local, and tribal governments, the private sector, nongovernmental organizations, and community partners to find innovative and atypical means to solve problems, and to obtain and apply resources that are not part of the normal process. Many of the most important needs are confronted during the initial hours of a response and are required by the populations most vulnerable in times of crisis.

Recovery is an opportunity for communities to rebuild in a manner that will reduce or eliminate risk from future incidents. Communities can incorporate stronger building codes and land-use ordinances. Vulnerable structures can be retrofitted, elevated, or removed from harm. Community members, businesses, and local governments can incorporate risk reductions strategies into governance and local decision making.

Most Americans are steadfast and resilient in times of crisis and can be an immediate and valuable resource for incident managers. FEMA's incident management and support operations should take that into account and empower survivors to participate in the response and recovery efforts.

TENET 2: EMPOWER EMERGENCY MANAGERS TO MAKE DECISIONS AND TAKE COORDINATED ACTION

The coordinated actions of the entire response community—not the efforts of any single individual or organization, no matter how bold—determine the success or failure of response operations. Emergency managers at the incident must be empowered to make decisions and perform their roles independently.

Responding to disasters and emergencies is a complex process because the operational environment is inherently extraordinary. For incidents that are large enough to require Federal support, the problems are even more complex. For such incidents, no single

> **Empower People to Make Decisions and Take Action**
>
> With clearly defined priorities and objectives, emergency managers should be empowered to make decisions and take actions. They should ask the following questions:
> - Is it good for survivors?
> - Is it legal and ethical?
> - Is it something I am willing to be accountable for?
>
> If the answer to these questions is "Yes." action should be taken.

organization or individual possesses all the assets or answers. Instead, the combined efforts of all partners provide the power to address critical needs and allow for an effective response and recovery.

To empower emergency managers, leaders must build a foundation of trust across the whole community, provide a clear vision for the operation, and treat all stakeholders as valued members of the team. The experience, expertise, and judgment of emergency managers should be leveraged to help tackle complex situations.

Emergency managers must be comfortable with uncertainty, innovative in solving problems, and willing to make decisions with less-than-perfect information and insufficient time. Decisions can be made by considering what is legal, moral, and best for survivors.

FEMA's role in response and recovery is unique. While other Federal departments and agencies may respond on their own and provide much-needed assistance, it is FEMA's job to identify, acquire, and deploy the necessary assets from across the Federal Government. FEMA must bring all of these Federal assets to bear on the situation quickly and effectively while ensuring that efforts are accomplished in coordination with State, local, and tribal officials and with private-sector and NGO response elements.

Unity of effort means coordinating activities to achieve common objectives regardless of whether the participants are from the same organization. FEMA response and recovery operations routinely involve multiple organizations at the local, regional, and national levels. FEMA's incident management and support operations can be effective only if they are implemented in a unified manner with our partners, to include Federal, State, local, tribal governments, the private sector, NGOs, communities, and individuals.

TENET 3: RESPOND QUICKLY WITH DECISIVE INITIAL ACTIONS

During a response to, and recovery from, any incident, the first decisions and actions that emergency managers and response personnel take set the stage for the success or failure of the response, and affect how costly and timely the recovery will be. Decisive effort must be exerted during the initial response.

Emergency managers must operate with a bias towards vital action and sometimes assume risk by making decisions in an environment of insufficient information. Emergency managers must constantly anticipate the worst-case scenario, determine which aspects of the incident are critical to success, and not hesitate to take action.

Emergency managers often confront problems that offer few attractive options. Speed, legality, cost, cultural sensitivities, ensuring the safety of and improving the lives of survivors—all are criteria that must be weighed. Speed and taking care of survivors are the most important criteria and should carry the heaviest weight in the decision-making process. A more deliberative decision-making process used in normal day-to-day operations may need to be put aside in order to save and sustain life and protect property. An imperfect action applied in time—and based on professional training, experience, and judgment—is better than a perfect solution applied too late.

Planning is a critical tool in reducing the amount of risk that is assumed during an initial response. It is also vital for integration, identification, and prioritization of key actions and projects in community recovery. Successful planning enhances emergency managers' ability to make decisions by providing potential courses of action and other key information.

> ## "THINK SMART. . . THINK BIG. . . GO BIG . . . GO FAST."
>
> FEMA personnel must focus on responding aggressively to every incident. We must do the following:
>
> - Always plan to support the communities, irrespective of the limitations that may inhibit us prior to an incident.
>
> - Quickly bring all possible resources to bear against the effects of an incident. In incident response, it is better to *have* and not want, than to *want* and not have.
>
> - Focus on stabilizing the incident during initial response, since effective response and recovery systems cannot be established without the requisite security.
>
> - Use experience, training, expertise, and judgment to make timely decisions when the necessary information is not available.

TENET 4: USE OUTCOME-BASED OBJECTIVES

Management by objective is a key characteristic of the National Incident Management System (NIMS). Clearly defined objectives that focus on outcomes—which measure *change*, rather than *outputs* (which measure numbers)—should drive all response activities. At every level of response, objectives focus actions toward achieving desired ends. This precept highlights the importance of having good objectives that enable responders to concentrate on the most important tasks and promote individual initiative and creativity.

Outcome-based objectives clarify what emergency managers need to accomplish by emphasizing the desired result rather than the method or intervening steps. An outcome-based objective would state, "Ensure that survivors have the basic commodities they need." A less effective, output-based objective would state, "Deliver 100 truckloads of bottled water." Response actions must focus on outcomes in terms of saving and sustaining life while supporting community resilience.

Similarly, a critical component of recovery is the establishment of realistic metrics for tracking progress, ensuring accountability, and reinforcing realistic expectations among stakeholders. Measuring and communicating the progress of recovery efforts increases public confidence in the recovery process by promoting transparency, accountability, and efficiency. It enables local leadership to identify ongoing recovery needs and engages partners in providing assistance and problem resolution. Recovery progress serves as a tracking mechanism for improving and adjusting recovery strategies and activities and ensuring continuing improvement.

> ## *Outputs* vs. *Outcomes*: An Example
>
> FEMA regularly provides massive amounts of commodities to the Agency's partners as well as to survivors. However, success is not measured in the volume of commodities moved.
>
> During a hurricane, FEMA could provide millions of liters of water to partners. If measured in *output*, the operation would be successful. However, if the water cannot be distributed due to environmental considerations, then the operation was still incomplete—when looked at in terms of *outcomes* (in this case, people having water).

Communities determine how to qualify and quantify their progress. They measure progress toward recovery holistically, recognizing that recovery outcomes and impacts are measured beyond a single criterion, such as dollars spent or assistance delivered on a program-by-program basis.

TENET 5: DEVELOP CREATIVE SOLUTIONS AND ATYPICAL RESOURCES

Response and recovery operations must be able to adapt and develop new systems and capabilities when existing capabilities are either destroyed or found to be inadequate to meet incident management and support requirements.

While hundreds of incidents occur each year, occasionally a disaster will strike that is of such proportions that it affects the entire Nation. Such catastrophes are characterized as follows:

- The effects of the incident overwhelm not only the standard governmental and economic processes but also the systems designed to operate during and in response to disasters.

- Requirements exceed available resources throughout the Nation.

- The incident otherwise profoundly affects the entire Nation. While all disasters are catastrophic to those whom they affect directly, some impact people across the country and may require response and recovery support from jurisdictions far beyond the borders of the affected State.

In such large-scale response and recovery operations, typical systems and resources may not offer the range of options needed to meet the requirements of survivors. Emergency managers may not be able to apply traditional solutions in ways that meet the requirements. Innovative thinking will be of utmost importance to meet the needs of survivors in large-scale events.

For incidents that can be anticipated, pre-disaster preparedness, planning, mitigation, and efforts in building community capacity and resilience are the key. Identifying the breaking point of our current systems and resources and comparing them to the anticipated needs enables us to plan ways to bridge the gaps. Building or acquiring needed capabilities is best done before a specific threat is realized. These efforts result in a resilient community with an improved capacity to respond and recover from future disasters. Timely decisions in response to these impacts can significantly reduce the cost and time for recovery.

Effective response and recovery operations in catastrophes represent a significant departure from response activities during routine incidents. In the aftermath of a catastrophe, FEMA emergency managers may not be able to rely on processes and procedures that work effectively in other incidents. Emergency managers at all levels, including FEMA personnel, will need to deal with the reality that all normal resources will already have been exhausted or unavailable; and they will need to apply their best experience and knowledge to find innovative ways to anticipate and meet the lifesaving and life-sustaining needs of State, local and tribal governments. In terms of acquiring and applying resources, these officials will need to respond quickly with decisive initial actions.

Logistics, in terms of getting what is needed to those who need it when they need it, is always a key issue in effective response; however, logistics takes on a life-or-death dimension in catastrophes. In catastrophes, the effects of the incident may incapacitate or overwhelm State and local governments, the private sector, and NGOs. In such situations, FEMA personnel must be prepared to act beyond their normal roles and quickly assume the responsibilities of these organizations and perform them effectively and efficiently—until the organizations can resume operations. Leaders must be prepared for other challenges, including management of expectations and the inevitability of external criticism of response and recovery efforts.

Finally, a catastrophic disaster is an opportunity to build a stronger more resilient community that is cognizant of sustainable community principles. By understanding the cause of damages, communities are able to take action to ensure rebuilding will reduce impacts of disasters in the future.

CHAPTER 5: FEMA INCIDENT MANAGEMENT AND SUPPORT KEY CONCEPTS

FEMA Incident Management and Support Key Concepts

1. Incident Management and Support are Conducted in Accordance with the National Incident Management System (NIMS).

2. Effective Preparedness Provides the Basis for Successful Incident Management and Support.

3. Incidents Are Categorized by Disaster Levels to Guide Deployment of Resources.

4. Incidents Should Be Managed at the Lowest Possible Operational Level.

5. Unity of Effort in Response Is Achieved Through Unified Command. Unity of Effort in Recovery is Achieved Through Unity of Purpose.

6. Disciplined Priorities Enable Meaningful Objectives.

7. Establishing a Secure Operating Environment, Including Emergency Routes, Is Essential to Effective Incident Management and Support.

8. Disaster Emergency Communications Are Essential to Effective Incident Management and Support.

9. Anticipate Potential Requirements and Quickly Move Resources to Support the Response and Short-Term Recovery.

10. Enable Citizens and Survivors to Assist Their Communities Before, During, and After an Incident.

11. Response and Recovery Actions Must Be Targeted to Assist the Most Vulnerable.

12. Response, Recovery, and Mitigation Activities Operate Concurrently as Part of Incident Management and Support.

13. Response and Recovery Decisions Are Informed By Risk Analysis

14. Planning Is the Foundation for Achieving Common Objectives Through Integrated Response and Recovery Efforts.

15. Successful Incident Management and Support Is Ultimately Accomplished When Communities Are More Resilient and Sustainable Than They Were Before the Incident.

16. Incident Planning Is a Key Activity at All Levels of FEMA Response Operations.

17. There Is Only One Incident Action Plan (IAP) for Each Incident, and the IAP Is Developed Only at the Incident Level.

18. Effective Incident Planning Requires a Comprehensive System for Information Collection, Sharing, and Analysis that Includes All Echelons of FEMA Response and Recovery Efforts.

19. Deliberate Planning Is the Foundation for Incident Planning.

20. Deliberate Planning Is Only as Effective as Its Ability to Guide Actual Operations.

Key concepts are the critical means through which incident management and support is accomplished. In support of tenets, these key concepts describe essential ideas, practices, and standards that must be followed in order to promote a unified and effective incident management and support. While not all of the concepts may apply to all situations, these concepts are the first bridge between theory and practice, between belief and action. They make tangible the ideas put forward in our tenets, as well as the principles as put forth in the National Response Framework (NRF). These concepts are intended to guide the development and conduct of operations, plans, training, staffing, equipping, and other contributors to successful incident management and support operations. Key concepts are the building blocks of successful operations.

CONCEPT 1: INCIDENT MANAGEMENT AND SUPPORT ARE CONDUCTED IN ACCORDANCE WITH NIMS

The National Incident Management System (NIMS) was developed to enhance the ability to manage domestic incidents within the United States. The objective is to ensure that all levels of government across the Nation work efficiently and effectively together, using a single, national approach to domestic incident management. NIMS provides a common incident management template that gives personnel a flexible but standardized system for emergency management and incident management and support activities. NIMS operational guidelines allow disparate organizations and agencies to work together in a coordinated manner.

A fundamental premise of NIMS is that incidents are typically managed at the local level *first*. NIMS is predicated on the concept that local jurisdictions retain command, control, and authority over response activities for their jurisdictional areas. Adhering to NIMS processes allows local agencies to better

---

What Is FEMA's *Incident Level*?

- While FEMA has commonly referred to it as "the field," FEMA's **incident level** refers to the level at which FEMA incident management is accomplished, typically in partnership with States and in support of local officials. This is the level at which a Unified Coordination Group (UCG) employs Federal resources to achieve jointly-developed incident objectives.

- The FEMA representative to the UCG is the Federal Coordinating Officer (FCO), who holds directive authority over FEMA assets. For a non-Stafford Act incident, the Department of Homeland Security (DHS) representative to the UCG is the Federal Coordinator.

- The area of a FEMA incident is defined by the geographical boundaries of the jurisdictions listed in the pertinent declaration in the case of a Stafford Act incident or other executive guidance for a non-Stafford Act incident.

- A Federal employee assigned as part of a command and general staff in support of a UCG operates under the roles and responsibilities of the incident position and under the authority of the leadership of the command and general Staff.

control and utilize incoming resources. Control is delegated to the lowest level of execution because the FEMA response element closest to the scene has the most direct knowledge of the situation, ready access to State and local officials, the capacity to apply resources with greatest accuracy, and the ability to adjust support quickly as needs change. Managing at the lowest level allows the incident objectives to be set at the operational level most acquainted with the needs of the affected population. This approach focuses the efforts of higher echelons within FEMA on the incident requirements and ensures unity of effort.

The Unified Coordination Group (UCG) is the primary Federal or State organizational structure for managing and supporting disaster response operations at the field level. Until a Federal Coordinating Officer (FCO) is appointed and establishes operational capability, the FEMA Region continues to coordinate Federal assistance to respond to the incident. This reduces unnecessary delay between incident occurrence and the initiation of a Federal response, should one be needed. After the establishment of a UCG, the Region maintains responsibility to support incident management. The role of FEMA headquarters is to support the affected Region(s).

The components of NIMS—(1) preparedness, (2) communications and information management, (3) resource management, (4) command and management, and (5) ongoing management and maintenance—were designed to work together flexibly and systematically to provide the national template for incident management.

NIMS integrates best practices into a comprehensive template for emergency management and response personnel to use nationwide in an all-hazards context. These best practices lay the groundwork for the components of NIMS and provide the mechanisms for the further development and refinement of the supporting national standards, guidelines, protocols, systems, and technologies. NIMS fosters the development of specialized technologies that facilitate emergency management and incident response activities, and allows for the adoption of new approaches that will enable continuous refinement of the system over time.

NIMS is not an operational incident management or resource allocation plan. NIMS is a core set of doctrines, concepts, principles, terminology, and organizational processes that enables effective, efficient, and collaborative incident management. To that end, FEMA doctrine is how FEMA operates within the NIMS operating systems.

All of the NIMS components are important to efficient response operations, but three apply directly to supporting an incident, as follows:

- Communications and information management
- Resource management
- Command and management

The function and importance of these three components are further explained below.

Communications and Information Management

Effective incident management and support activities rely on flexible, reliable communications and information systems that provide situational awareness to emergency management and response personnel and their affiliated organizations. Properly planned and executed communications systems enable the dissemination of information among command and support elements and, as appropriate, cooperating agencies and organizations.

Incident communications require the development and use of common communications plans and interoperable communications equipment, processes, standards, and architectures. During an incident, this integrated approach links the operational and support units of the various organizations. Communications and information management planning address the incident-related policies, equipment, systems, standards, and training necessary to achieve integrated communications.

Situational awareness is established and maintained by collecting, analyzing, and disseminating incident information to all appropriate parties. The following characteristics facilitate situational awareness:

- **Interoperability** allows emergency management and response personnel to communicate within and across agencies and jurisdictions via voice, data, or video, when needed and when authorized

- **Reliability** enables communications and information systems to function in any type of incident and under adverse conditions

- **Scalability** allows responders to increase the number of users in a system

- **Portability** permits communications and information systems to move easily and quickly

- **Resiliency** enables communication systems to withstand and continue to perform after damage or infrastructure loss

- **Redundancy** ensures that there are always multiple means to communicate

Resource Management

Incident management and support activities require the skillful management of resources (personnel, teams, facilities, equipment, and/or supplies) to meet incident needs. Typing, inventorying, organizing, and tracking facilitate the ordering, deployment, and recovery or demobilization of resources before, during, and after an incident.

Resource management includes the coordination, oversight, and other processes that provide the right resources when and where they are needed. Resources are ordered to meet identified needs based on evolving incident priorities. As an incident grows in size or complexity, or if it starts on a large scale, other sources—Federal, State, the private sector, and nongovernmental organizations (NGOs)—may have to meet resource needs.

Efficient and effective deployment of resources requires that sound resource management concepts and principles be used in all phases of emergency management and incident response. The underlying concepts of resource management are the following:

- **Consistency:** A standard method for identifying, acquiring, allocating, and tracking resources

- **Standardization:** Resource typing, which includes naming conventions, to improve the effectiveness of resource ordering

- **Coordination:** Facilitation and integration of resources for optimal benefit

- **Use:** Incorporating resources from all levels of government, the private sector, and NGOs, where appropriate, in resource management planning efforts

- **Information management:** Thorough integration of communications and information management elements into resource management organizations, processes, technologies, and decision support

- **Credentialing:** Use of criteria that ensure consistent training, licensure, and certification standards

It is incumbent upon emergency managers to be able to develop response and recovery capabilities, preferably through capabilities-based planning before an event, to address requirements for which resources do not exist. During the response to and recovery from catastrophes, the needs of communities and survivors will not be met through government assets alone. Through the innovative and adaptive application of our Nation's capabilities, both public and private, we can and will enable our communities to respond to and recover from these incidents.

Command and Management—The Incident Command System and Multiagency Coordination System

The Incident Command System (ICS) is designed to manage incidents. While the management characteristics of ICS apply to FEMA operations at all levels, FEMA uses the actual ICS organization and functions at the incident level only.

Flexibility to manage incidents of any size requires coordination and standardization among emergency management and response personnel and their affiliated organizations. At the heart of NIMS is ICS, which standardizes key incident management characteristics such as modular organization, common terminology, manageable span of control, unity of command and chain of command, incident action planning, and comprehensive resource management. All of these promote common understanding and integration among jurisdictions and disciplines. All levels of government—Federal, State, tribal, and local—as well as many NGOs and the private sector use ICS at the incident level. As a system, ICS not only provides an organizational structure for incident management but also guides the process for planning, building, and adapting that structure.

ICS Management Characteristics

1. Common terminology
2. Modular organization
3. Management by objectives
4. Incident action planning
5. Manageable span of control
6. Incident facilities and locations
7. Comprehensive resource management
8. Integrated communications
9. Establishment and transfer of command
10. Chain of command and unity of command
11. Unified command
12. Accountability
13. Dispatch and deployment
14. Information and intelligence management

ICS is designed to be adaptable, flexible, and scalable in order to function in any type of incident, regardless of cause, size, location, or complexity—and whether the incident is within a single jurisdiction or agency, a single jurisdiction with multiagency involvement, or multiple jurisdictions with multiagency involvement. As incidents change in size, scope, and complexity, the response must be adaptable to meet changing requirements. Execution must be flexible and adapted to specifically fit the nature and scope of a given incident.

The implementation of ICS corresponds to the size and complexity of the incident. Selective implementation allows for a scaled response and a level of coordination appropriate to each event. It is not always obvious whether a seemingly minor incident might be the initial phase of a larger, rapidly growing threat. Response and recovery must be quickly adaptable, flexible, and scalable.

A common misunderstanding is that in being adaptable, flexible, and scalable, ICS can be whatever an individual or organization wants it to be. But NIMS and ICS are standardized systems. In the context of ICS, *adaptable*, *flexible*, and *scalable* are defined as follows:

- **Adaptable** means that ICS can be used to manage any kind or type of hazard or incident that may be the threat or occurrence of either a natural or man-made disaster or a planned event, such as the Olympics.

- **Flexible** means that the organizational structure is a modular design, which allows the flexibility of using only the organizational response functions required for the incident. However, the Operations Section must always be the focus of an ICS structure.

- **Scalable** means that the ICS can expand to fit the magnitude of the incident, from a very small incident to a large complex incident. This characteristic allows only the necessary positions to be staffed based on incident needs.

Nothing that the terms *adaptable*, *flexible*, and *scalable* describe permits organizations to ignore the 14 ICS Management Characteristics inherent to ICS. The organizational structure can be expanded or reduced. New positions can be created to meet the needs of the incident as long as the changes conform to the organizational protocols and the ICS management characteristics. Functioning in accordance with NIMS improves FEMA response operations by applying tested incident management concepts, and improves FEMA's capacity to interface efficiently and effectively with State, local, NGO, and private-sector partners.

Using ICS for every incident or planned event hones the skills needed for the large-scale incidents. Failing to consistently utilize ICS degrades an organization's ability to respond effectively.

Our accepted mechanisms for command and coordination may not be available for use during the initial stages of a catastrophe. FEMA's emergency management professionals must be ready to operate in this type of austere environment by applying effective planning, marshaling as robust a response capability as possible, and using judgment in applying these resources in an information-deprived environment. Most leaders will be able to command and control only those facets of a response with which they are physically collocated and where they can control the outcomes. All efforts will need to be focused on the priorities of saving and sustaining lives, and every effort must be made to capitalize on available resources to maximize the support provided.

The Multiagency Coordination System (MACS) is a process that allows all levels of government and all disciplines to work together more efficiently and effectively. Multiagency coordination occurs across the different disciplines involved in incident management, across jurisdictional lines, or across levels of government. Multiagency coordination can and does occur regularly whenever personnel from different agencies interact in such activities as preparedness, prevention, response, recovery, and mitigation.

CONCEPT 2: EFFECTIVE PREPAREDNESS PROVIDES THE BASIS FOR SUCCESSFUL INCIDENT MANAGEMENT AND SUPPORT

Effective disaster response and recovery operations are based on preparedness, which includes a continuous cycle of planning, organizing, training, equipping, exercising, evaluating, and taking corrective action. Preparedness efforts validate and maintain plans, policies, and procedures, describing how they will prioritize, coordinate, and manage information and resources.

- Planning builds relationships, provides the tools for capability building, identifies resources, and outlines operational and organizational concepts that are the fundamental building blocks for effective response and recovery operations.

- Training and equipping provide personnel with the knowledge, skills, and tools they need to perform their assigned functions as an individual or as part of a defined team.

- Conducting exercises allows individuals and teams to rehearse and demonstrate capabilities.

- Assessing and evaluating performance in actual incidents and exercises provides an empirical basis for improving plans and capabilities.

Preparedness activities must be coordinated among all appropriate agencies, organizations, and Federal, State, tribal, and local authorities. Well-established, pre-disaster partnerships at the local, tribal, State and Federal levels help to drive a successful response and recovery process. Individual, business, and community preparation and resilience-building programs provide a foundation for recovery plans that improve the speed and quality of post-disaster recovery decisions.

CONCEPT 3: INCIDENTS ARE CATEGORIZED BY DISASTER LEVELS TO GUIDE DEPLOYMENT OF RESOURCES

FEMA uses three disaster levels (figure 1) to categorize an incident based on the actual or anticipated impact, size, complexity of the incident, and the Federal assistance required. The Director of Disaster Operations (DDO) and FEMA Regional Administrator (RA) coordinate on the designation of disaster levels and may adjust disaster level designations as the magnitude and complexity of the incident change.[2] They will use these designations to guide the assignment of resources such as Incident Management Assistance Teams (IMATs)—that are, Type I, II, or III.

LEVEL I

- *An incident of such magnitude that the available assets that were designed and put in place for the response are completely overwhelmed or broken at the local, regional, or national level.*

- *Due to its severity, size, location, actual or potential impact on public health, welfare, and infrastructure it requires an extreme amount of federal assistance for response and recovery efforts for which the capabilities to support do not exist at any level of government.*

- *A Level I Disaster requires extraordinary coordination among federal, state, tribal, and local entities due to massive levels and breadth of damage, severe impact or multi-State scope.*

- *Major involvement of FEMA (full activation of RRCC and NRCC), other federal agencies (all primary Emergency Support Function (ESF) agencies activated), and deployment of initial response resources are required to support requirements of the affected State.*

LEVEL II

- *A disaster which, due to its severity, size, location, actual or potential impact on public health, welfare, and infrastructure requires a high amount of direct federal assistance for response and recovery efforts.*

- *A Level II Disaster requires elevated coordination among federal, state, tribal, and local entities due to moderate levels and breadth of damage.*

- *Significant involvement of FEMA (RRCC activation, possible NRCC activation), other federal agencies (some ESF primary agencies activated to support RRCC), and possible deployment of initial response resources are required to support requirements of the affected State.*

LEVEL III

- *A disaster which, due to its severity, size, location, actual or potential impact on public health, welfare, and infrastructure requires a moderate amount of direct federal assistance.*

- *Typically this is primarily a recovery effort with minimal response requirements and existing federal and regional resources will meet requests.*

- *A Level III Disaster requires coordination among involved federal, state, tribal, and local entities due to minor-to-average levels and breadth of damage. Federal assistance may be limited to activation of only one or two ESF primary agencies.*

Figure 1. FEMA Disaster Levels

---

[2] The role of the DDO is to synchronize all FEMA Headquarters response operations and related activities during major disasters or emergency activations. "Headquarters Leadership During Disaster Operations," FEMA Administrator memorandum, June 25, 2009.

Resources are organized by category, kind, and type, including size, capacity, capability, skill, and other characteristics. This makes the resource ordering among all levels of governments, NGOs, and the private sector more efficient and ensures that communities receive needed resources.

In a catastrophic (Level I) incident, FEMA officials must anticipate that many needed resources will simply not be available. Meeting critical shortfalls will require both innovation and tapping nontraditional sources.

CONCEPT 4: INCIDENTS SHOULD BE MANAGED AT THE LOWEST POSSIBLE OPERATIONAL LEVEL

A basic premise of NIMS and the NRF is that incidents should be managed at the lowest possible level.

Control of FEMA incident management and support efforts is delegated to the lowest level of execution because the FEMA element closest to the scene has the most direct knowledge of the situation, most ready access to State and local officials, the capacity to employ resources with greatest accuracy, and the ability to adjust support quickly as needs change. Delegating control in this way emphasizes a bottom-up approach to the chain of command, from the incident through the Region to FEMA Headquarters.

Delegating control enables officials at various levels and with different authorities and responsibilities to organize, plan, and assign resources necessary to accomplish incident objectives and prioritize recovery actions and projects.

> **We manage incidents at the lowest operational level because FEMA personnel closest to the scene**
> - have the most direct knowledge of the situation,
> - have the most ready access to State and local officials,
> - have the capacity to apply resources with the greatest precision, and
> - can adjust activities and resources quickly as needs change.

The FEMA Administrator and Regional Administrator; State, tribal, and local emergency response organizations; and other Federal and private-sector agencies maintain control of their assigned resources until they choose to delegate that control. The FEMA Administrator and RAs may delegate control of FEMA-specific resources to the FCO when the FCO is ready to take charge; that delegation can be rescinded as necessary. Once the FCO has control, the FCO directs Federal resources, as required, to accomplish incident objectives. The FCO may allow other Federal, State, tribal, or local incident commanders to temporarily control and direct FEMA resources, but the FCO or appropriate Federal authorities always retain final control of Federal resources.

Concept 5: Unity of Effort in Response Is Achieved Through Unified Command. Unity of Effort in Recovery is Achieved Through Unity of Purpose

Successful incident management and support operations require unity of effort.

Cooperation and mutual aid are the cornerstones of success for effective joint activity. A coordinated approach that promotes unity of effort provides the strongest foundation to manage all hazards and threats. Unity of effort is achieved through clearly defined roles and responsibilities, access to information, and a shared understanding of how risks are managed and prioritized to inform the allocation of limited resources.

Clear, objectively measurable, collaboratively developed performance metrics help define collective unity of purpose. Unity of purpose is the foundation for unity of effort during incident management and support operations.

Unified command is a structure that brings together the designated officials from the principal jurisdictions affected by the incident to coordinate an effective response while carrying out their own jurisdictional responsibilities. Unified command ensures that, regardless of the number of agencies or jurisdictions involved, all decisions are based on mutually agreed-upon objectives.

FEMA incident management activities are organized at the incident level according to the ICS structure. Unity of effort is achieved through the UCG—the structure that executes unified command and leads incident activities. The UCG is composed of senior leaders representing Federal and State interests, and, in certain circumstances, tribal governments, local jurisdictions, and/or the private sector. The FCO is the primary Federal official responsible for coordinating, integrating, and synchronizing Federal response activities in Stafford Act incidents. The FCO is also responsible for establishing the UCG, the composition of which varies from incident to incident depending on the scope and nature of the disaster and the assets needed. A UCG enables agencies with different legal, geographic, and functional authorities and responsibilities to coordinate, plan, and interact effectively.

The ICS organization is not appropriate to use at levels other than the incident. However, this does not mean that unified command is impossible. For support activities such as those conducted in the Regional and National Response Coordination Centers, unity of effort and unified command are achieved through an alternative structure that is consistent with the principles of NIMS and ICS. MACs is the structure that facilitates unified command beyond the incident level.

While the UCG provides the mechanism for coordinating public response, it must also reach out and embrace private entities that have and will continue to ensure the viability of communities before and after an incident. We must not seek to replicate private systems, but include them as a function that must be enabled.

Multiagency Coordination System (MACS). The principal functions and responsibilities of MACS entities typically include ensuring that each agency involved in incident management activities is providing appropriate situational awareness and resource status information; establishing priorities between incidents and/or area commands in concert with the Incident Coordination Group or UCG(s); acquiring and allocating resources required by incident management personnel in concert with the priorities established by the UCG(s); anticipating and identifying future resource requirements; coordinating and resolving policy issues arising from the incident(s); and providing strategic coordination as required.

While FEMA's response and recovery efforts center around the incident level, FEMA's regional and national elements have important capabilities and expertise that are applied to support the UCG. At the national level, FEMA Headquarters officials interface with senior Presidential Administration personnel, the leaders of other DHS components, other Federal departments and agencies, the private sector, and NGOs to expedite resources and find solutions to policy and programmatic problems that are impeding response and recovery. At the FEMA regional level, the FEMA RA is ultimately responsible for the FEMA response to all incidents in the region. Regional response and recovery coordination and program division staff in the Regional offices represent the first line of support to the FCO and UCG by helping to source and deploy required resources.

Catastrophes may render traditional incident command structures and even the normal unified command processes impractical. In such cases, leaders must be prepared to operate promptly and, in some cases, *unilaterally*—based on priorities and the best information available with regard to needs.

Unity of Purpose Through Community and Partner Engagement. A key element in an expedient recovery involves community interface and successful coordination with outside sources of help, such as surrounding governments, foundations, universities, nonprofit organizations, and private-sector entities.

Recovery stakeholders leverage and coordinate disaster and traditional public- and private-assistance programs to accelerate the recovery process and to avoid duplication of efforts.

Leadership establishes the guidance for the transition from response operations to recovery and, finally, a return to a normal state of community functioning, including the shift of roles and responsibilities.

Stakeholders collaborate to maximize the use of available resources to rebuild housing, infrastructure, schools, businesses, and the social-historical-cultural fabric of the impacted community in a resilient manner. Collaboration of stakeholders is also necessary to provide health care access and functional support services. Local opinions are incorporated so that community needs are met in a more holistic manner, maximizing the provision and utilization of recovery resources. All perspectives within the community have an opportunity to participate in all phases of disaster and recovery planning; transparency and accountability in the process are clearly evident. Impacted communities assume the leadership in developing recovery priorities and activities that are realistic, well-planned, and clearly communicated.

Organizational structures for coordinating recovery assistance are scalable and flexible. Recovery structures at all government levels evolve, adapt, and develop new skills and capacities to address the changing landscape of post-disaster environments.

CONCEPT 6: DISCIPLINED PRIORITIES ENABLE MEANINGFUL OBJECTIVES

It is critical during the initial response to an event for action priorities to be established. Priorities give precedence to incident objectives, and while objectives must be based on requirements, priorities guide the status in which objectives must be addressed.

During a large-scale or complex event, resources and capabilities will not exist to meet all competing demands. A disciplined set of response and recovery priorities is crucial in order to communicate to all those involved in incident management and support what must be accomplished first. This is especially crucial for resources and capabilities that are in high demand—and few of which may exist—during an incident. Emergency managers can use priorities to guide the employment of resources in support of objectives.

CONCEPT 7: ESTABLISHING A SECURE OPERATING ENVIRONMENT, INCLUDING EMERGENCY ROUTES, IS ESSENTIAL TO EFFECTIVE INCIDENT MANAGEMENT AND SUPPORT

Ensuring the safety and security of survivors and emergency workers is a fundamental requirement. Failure to establish and maintain a secure environment will hinder all response efforts.

- Effective incident management and support activities rely on clear access to the disaster scene, flexible and reliable communications, and information systems that provide situational awareness to emergency management and response personnel and their affiliated organizations.

- Effective response requires that response officials can get resources (responders, teams, equipment, and commodities) to those affected by the incident. FEMA must support local efforts to clear highways, bridges, ports, and airports as a first priority in incident management and support operations. Without the capacity to get the needed resources to disaster survivors, response efforts cannot succeed.

CONCEPT 8: DISASTER EMERGENCY COMMUNICATIONS ARE ESSENTIAL TO EFFECTIVE INCIDENT MANAGEMENT AND SUPPORT

Establishing and maintaining effective disaster emergency communications and information systems is critical to FEMA's role in coordinating the Federal government's response, continuity efforts, and restoration of essential services before, during, and after an incident. Promoting and providing operable and interoperable communications and information systems capabilities across all levels of government ensures mission-critical information and situational awareness for emergency management decision-makers and support elements.

Ensuring effective incident communications requires the following:

- Supporting effective, tactical, operable and interoperable voice, video, and information systems for emergency response teams

- Identifying and documenting mission-critical disaster emergency communications and information systems capabilities, requirements, solutions, and mitigation strategies

- Developing effective command and control communications frameworks

- Supporting the coordination and delivery of secure communications solutions

- Promoting communications interoperability with Federal, State, tribal, and local emergency response providers

CONCEPT 9: ANTICIPATE POTENTIAL REQUIREMENTS AND QUICKLY MOVE RESOURCES TO SUPPORT THE RESPONSE AND SHORT-TERM RECOVERY

Resource management consists of the coordination, oversight, and processes that provide timely and appropriate resources during an incident. As incident priorities are established, the needs are identified and the resources ordered. Management systems function to translate incident resource requests into actual delivered materiel and capability where and when needed.

To ensure rapid response to a disaster, FEMA may proactively alert its Logistics Distribution Centers before an incident occurs; identify and set up mobilization centers and staging areas (in the vicinity of the affected area); and begin deploying

Pushing Resources

Pushing resources is the process of FEMA incident support officials dispatching pre-planned individuals, teams, equipment, and supplies to convenient but non-intrusive locations in the vicinity of the incident without a specific request from the incident level. From this location the UCG may apply the resources expeditiously to achieve incident objectives. Pushing resources is intended to meet critical needs promptly but not to overwhelm the staff at the incident with items they do not want or need.

commodities and teams based on predetermined execution schedules or resource-modeling tools. FEMA commodities remain under Federal control until transferred to a particular State.

The UCG, once operational, takes responsibility for identifying requirements, directing staging areas in or near the affected area, and coordinating logistical support for resources deployed to the affected area.

To expedite the availability of essential resources before or immediately after a disaster, commodities and teams may be pushed to the mobilization centers, Incident Support Bases, and staging areas. When commodities are pushed, clear communications with lower operational levels are essential to ensure that sufficient personnel and facilities are available to receive and manage them.

The process of pushing resources will transition to a *pull* process as soon as operational control is established at the incident level (for example, the RA ceases sending resources and the FCO begins requesting resources). The UCG then establishes resource requirements in coordination with State, territorial, and/or tribal partners.

As an exception to this established process, during a Type I incident when there is no lower level to task—due to the lack of communications or presence on the ground—FEMA national incident support officials may push resources from the whole of the Nation to the impacted area to meet anticipated needs.

CONCEPT 10: ENABLE CITIZENS AND SURVIVORS TO ASSIST THEIR COMMUNITIES BEFORE, DURING, AND AFTER AN INCIDENT

Both during and after disasters and emergencies, those who survive the incident are the first to respond, helping neighbors and others who have been affected even before first responders arrive. As the situation stabilizes, survivors continue to rally together to provide assistance. Local government should recognize members of the community as an important resource and work to enable their efforts before, during, and after an incident. FEMA supports State and local governments in encouraging survivor and citizen involvement in preparedness, response, recovery, and mitigation activities.

An Example of Engaging Citizens:

FEMA supports citizen engagement through initiatives such as Citizens Corps grants and Community Emergency Response Team (CERT) training.

CERT enhances community self-sufficiency through the development of multifunctional response teams who act as an adjunct to communities' emergency services during major disasters. When emergencies happen, CERT members can give critical support to first responders and safely provide immediate assistance to victims.

CONCEPT 11: RESPONSE AND RECOVERY ACTIONS MUST BE TARGETED TO ASSIST THE MOST VULNERABLE

While bold, coordinated action is called for in FEMA's response, it is critical to remember that the success of the response and community's recovery is going to be measured in how the most vulnerable members of the community are cared for. FEMA needs to assure that response and recovery activities respect the civil rights and civil liberties of all populations and do not result in discrimination on account of race, color, national origin (including limited English proficiency), religion, sex, or any form of disability.

The medically frail, the very young, the elderly, and persons with other special needs should be a primary focus during the response and recovery efforts. Leveraging the desire of local citizens to assist emergency managers will expand the resources available to maximize the support to this segment of the community and improve the effectiveness of the overall response and recovery.

CONCEPT 12: RESPONSE, RECOVERY, AND MITIGATION ACTIVITIES OPERATE CONCURRENTLY AS PART OF INCIDENT MANAGEMENT AND SUPPORT

All aspects of FEMA operations, programs, and activities are important to the people and communities affected by an incident. Response, recovery, and hazard mitigation often are concurrent (and not sequential) activities. Immediate actions to save lives, meet human needs, and protect property and the environment receives priority in the early stages of a disaster. However, even as these immediate imperatives are being addressed, recovery and mitigation efforts must begin.

While the initial emphasis may be on response, response actually happens concurrently with the execution of short-term recovery and the planning for long-term recovery. For example, individual assistance activities, such as providing shelters, registration, and information on registration; assessing locations for Disaster Recovery Centers; and assessing potential temporary housing needs—all require immediate attention. Some of these activities may be considered short-term recovery even though they persist for a longer term. Longer-term recovery programs such as public assistance and hazard mitigation normally begin before the immediate response activities are completed.

While various components of FEMA have specific programs or capabilities that can assist local jurisdictions in the aftermath of a disaster, the various FEMA components cannot apply these programs and capabilities independently. Instead, the efforts of all FEMA elements must be synchronized, and this is the responsibility of the "operations" function at the incident level. Regionally, ensuring the coordination of FEMA programs and capabilities to support the incident is the responsibility of the RA and the Regional Response Coordination

Staff. The FEMA Administrator is ultimately responsible for synchronizing incident support activities within FEMA, accomplishing this through the DDO and the National Response Coordination Staff.

CONCEPT 13: RESPONSE AND RECOVERY DECISIONS ARE INFORMED BY RISK ANALYSIS

Understanding how hazard characteristics affect communities is crucial to providing effective emergency response and informed recovery actions. By understanding natural and manmade hazards and how they can affect people, communities and the built environment, FEMA can make risk-informed decisions from the earliest response activity through sustained recovery actions. FEMA utilizes risk analysis tools to assist communities in evaluating and managing the risk posed by hazards, and coordinates Federal Response around sound risk information.

FEMA provides comprehensive risk management strategies by engaging public and private sector resources and partners to develop studies and maps of hazard information, assists in the development of community mitigation planning and use of real time data and predictive modeling during events to provide critical risk analysis. In addition, ongoing risk analysis is conducted through Risk Analysis programs at FEMA headquarters, regional program offices and field offices.

CONCEPT 14: PLANNING IS THE FOUNDATION FOR ACHIEVING COMMON OBJECTIVES THROUGH INTEGRATED RESPONSE AND RECOVERY EFFORTS

For FEMA response doctrine purposes, two fundamental types of emergency planning are established as follows:

- **Deliberate planning** is accomplished under nonemergency conditions, developing general procedures for responding to future threats or scenarios.

- **Incident planning** is associated with an actual or potential incident, likely under emergency conditions, developing procedures for responding to actual or projected effects. This includes Incident Action Planning and planning efforts described by terms such as crisis action planning, strategic planning, and adaptive/advanced planning.

For FEMA recovery doctrine purposes, two fundamental types of recovery planning are established, as follows:

- **Pre-disaster recovery planning** enables local, State, and tribal governments to effectively direct recovery activities and expedite a unified recovery effort. Pre-disaster plans provide a common platform to guide recovery decisions and activities. Pre-disaster recovery planning involves a State or community articulating a process for how it organizes and manages its long-term recovery, establishes relationships among stakeholders, and develops methods for prioritizing recovery decisions and addresses land-use considerations. Effective community pre-disaster recovery planning includes integration with other recovery preparedness, mitigation, and community resilience-building work. Individual, business, and community preparations and resilience-building provide a foundation for recovery plans that improve the speed and quality of post-disaster recovery decisions.

- **Post-disaster recovery planning** puts complex decisions in the context of the disaster and forms the foundation for allocating resources. The planning process provides the benchmark to measure the affected community's progress toward a successful outcome. Post-disaster recovery planning involves incorporating constituents' input, leading the development of the community's recovery visions, priorities, resources, capability, and capacity. Post-disaster recovery planning incorporates critical mitigation efforts as well as resilience, sustainability, and accessibility-building measures.

Proper pre- and post-disaster planning is critical for communities to develop resilience and is a prerequisite for the implementation of a well-constructed recovery process.

Planning is a foundational element of both preparedness and all phases of incident management and support. Planning benefits emergency management by doing the following:

- Identifying objectives
- Describing organization structure(s)
- Assigning tasks to achieve objectives
- Identifying resources to accomplish tasks
- Anticipating potential impediments and issues
- Contributing to unity of effort by providing a common blueprint for all incident management and incident support activities

Planning activities are based on the principles and tenets of the NRF. The planning process initiates and builds important personal relationships that add tremendous value during incident response and recovery operations.

CONCEPT 15: SUCCESSFUL INCIDENT MANAGEMENT AND SUPPORT IS ULTIMATELY ACCOMPLISHED WHEN COMMUNITIES ARE MORE RESILIENT AND SUSTAINABLE THAN THEY WERE BEFORE THE INCIDENT.

Resilient and sustainable communities are better able to respond to and recover from incidents. Federal efforts, as described in the Stafford Act and foundational documents to this keystone document, reinforce these principles at the community level by providing assistance for communities to reduce their risk from hazards. As a result, sound incident management and support incorporates recovery and mitigation throughout Federal efforts. Federal support to a community fosters risk analysis, risk reduction, and risk insurance principles and practices to assist communities throughout a disaster—to rebuild a safer and more resilient community through the delivery of Federal hazard mitigation assistance.

Resilience incorporates hazard mitigation strategies; critical infrastructure, environmental, and cultural resource protection; and sustainability practices—not only in reconstructing the built environment, such as housing and infrastructures, but also in revitalizing the economic, social, and natural environments. A successful Federal management and support role for response, recovery, and mitigation efforts will respond to immediate operational requirements, while at the same time facilitating a recovery that supports a more resilient community. Federal assistance programs for response, recovery, and mitigation have proven successful when they help communities reach these goals.

CONCEPT 16: INCIDENT PLANNING IS A KEY ACTIVITY AT ALL ECHELONS OF FEMA RESPONSE AND RECOVERY

Planning guides incident response and recovery operations at all levels and ensures that the focus remains on achieving incident objectives. Incident planning is an integral element of incident management and support and is thus a critical component of the response. This means that planning activities, whether developing situational awareness or creating planning products, must fulfill requirements that are closely coordinated with response staff members. Planners are facilitators who provide a coherent process to capture and articulate response concepts.

Incident planning rests on the foundation of deliberate planning, which outlines the roles, responsibilities, authorities, and resources of departments and agencies. Deliberate plans, which are developed pre-incident, are adapted to fit an actual incident. Both deliberate plans and incident plans must support State, local and tribal partners in addressing not only the average resident who may be affected by the disaster but also the whole community and the most vulnerable, including children, the elderly, other underserved populations, and those with special needs. Incident plans include the Incident Action Plan (IAP), Incident Functional Plans, the Advance Operational Plan (AOP), the Incident Strategic Plan, and Regional and National Support Plans, as well as functional plans that may be developed at any level.

In dealing with incidents of catastrophic proportions, traditional planning efforts may be insufficient. Regional and national support planning in such cases must address and resolve the critical resource shortfalls and logistical challenges that cannot be met through normal processes.

Planning is a key function at the incident, regional, and national levels; however, because incident management is done only at the incident level, planning done at the incident *support* levels (regional and national) is inherently different. The next section outlines the types of planning done at each level (also see table 1).

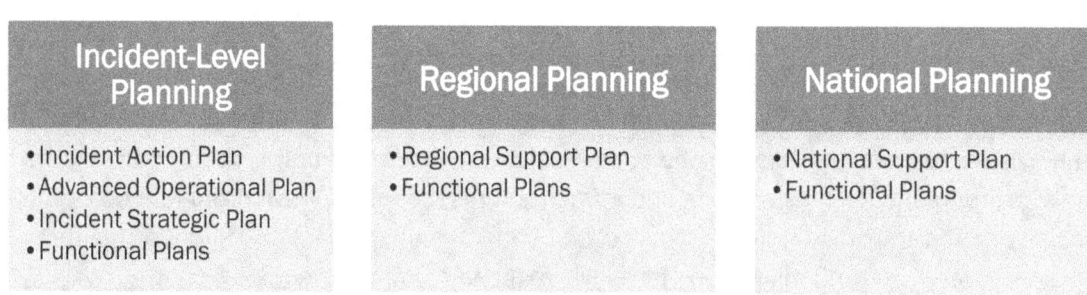

Incident-Level Planning	Regional Planning	National Planning
• Incident Action Plan • Advanced Operational Plan • Incident Strategic Plan • Functional Plans	• Regional Support Plan • Functional Plans	• National Support Plan • Functional Plans

Table 1: Incident Planning Levels

FEMA Incident-Level Planning

The UCG develops the incident objectives and is responsible for the following planning activities:

- Executing the incident command structure incident action planning process to produce an **IAP** for each operational period.
    - An IAP is a written document, and contains general objectives reflecting the strategy for managing an incident, which may include the identification of operational resources and assignments, attachments that provide direction, and important information for incident management.
    - The IAP is the focal point of incident-level planning. It builds on Federal, State, tribal, and local deliberate plans, tailoring efforts to the priorities and objectives established by the UCG.
    - The IAP will govern evolving operational periods throughout the life of the Federal response recovery and mitigation efforts.
- Developing and maintaining an **AOP** to estimate requirements and anticipate activities over multiple operational periods (typically three to seven days beyond the current operational period).
    - An **AOP** identifies and quantifies anticipated short-term critical resource requirements for operations (such as initial response resources, specialized teams, and aviation assets). The AOP is based on and supports incident objectives and priorities, and complements incident action planning. It includes short-term milestones that facilitate timely ordering to ensure that resources are available when needed.

- Additionally, the AOP provides a mechanism to synchronize other planning efforts beyond the current operational period, capture procedures derived from deliberate plans, and identify future resource requirements that may take longer to provide—or that will not be needed until later in the incident.

- Developing and maintaining an **Incident Strategic Plan** to estimate requirements and anticipate activities over the life cycle of the entire incident.

  - An **Incident Strategic Plan** is a written document that provides overall direction for incident management and specifies milestones to be accomplished over time. It outlines the goals, operational priorities, and desired end-state that enable the UCG to determine where they are in the life cycle of the incident and when goals have been achieved. Longer-term goals form the foundation of the Incident Strategic Plan, laying out where the UCG wants response and recovery and mitigation operations to be at selected times along a complete incident timeline. The UCG develops and approves these goals that are based on input from the command and general staff. The command and general staff then develop the milestones and estimated workload and staffing requirements.

- Developing **functional plans**, as necessary, to address particular operational issues, such as interim housing, power restoration, demobilization, and continuity of operations.

  - **Functional plans** are developed as required to address specific functional and operational issues. They are not confined to the current operational period but may address a single operational period or multiple operational periods. A functional plan will typically include identification of the operational resources required and proposed actions; it may also include timelines and milestones.

FEMA Regional Support Planning

The Regional Response Coordination Center Staff conducts planning at the regional level to provide regional resources and guidance to support incident operations. Regional planning may include the following:

- Developing a **regional support plan** that identifies the resources required to support the incident objectives and priorities. Possibly covering multiple operational periods, this process focuses and documents regional support efforts, and the resulting plan provides information to both the incident personnel and headquarters officials on regional efforts to support the incident. Regional support planning can identify resources available and assist in the development of AOPs by identifying gaps in critical assets.

- Developing **functional plans, as required,** to address particular requirements or emergent program policy issues (for example, regionally sharing disaster commodities or adjudicating individual assistance eligibility) in support of one or more incidents within the region.

FEMA National Support Planning

The National Response Coordination Center Staff conducts planning to support regional and incident operations. Headquarters planning may include the following:

- Developing a **national support plan** as needed to assist regional support and incident efforts when the Regional Response Coordination Center is not activated. This plan outlines national efforts to support incident and regional priorities. It provides information to the incident personnel, regional staff, and other senior leaders on national efforts to support the incident.

- Developing **functional plans** as *required*, addressing particular requirements or emergent program policy issues associated with one or more incidents. These plans outline specific national functional or programmatic efforts to support the incident.

Communication among the incident, regional, and national levels is essential to the success of incident planning at all levels. Figure 2 illustrates the time frames and roles of the four types of plans discussed above.

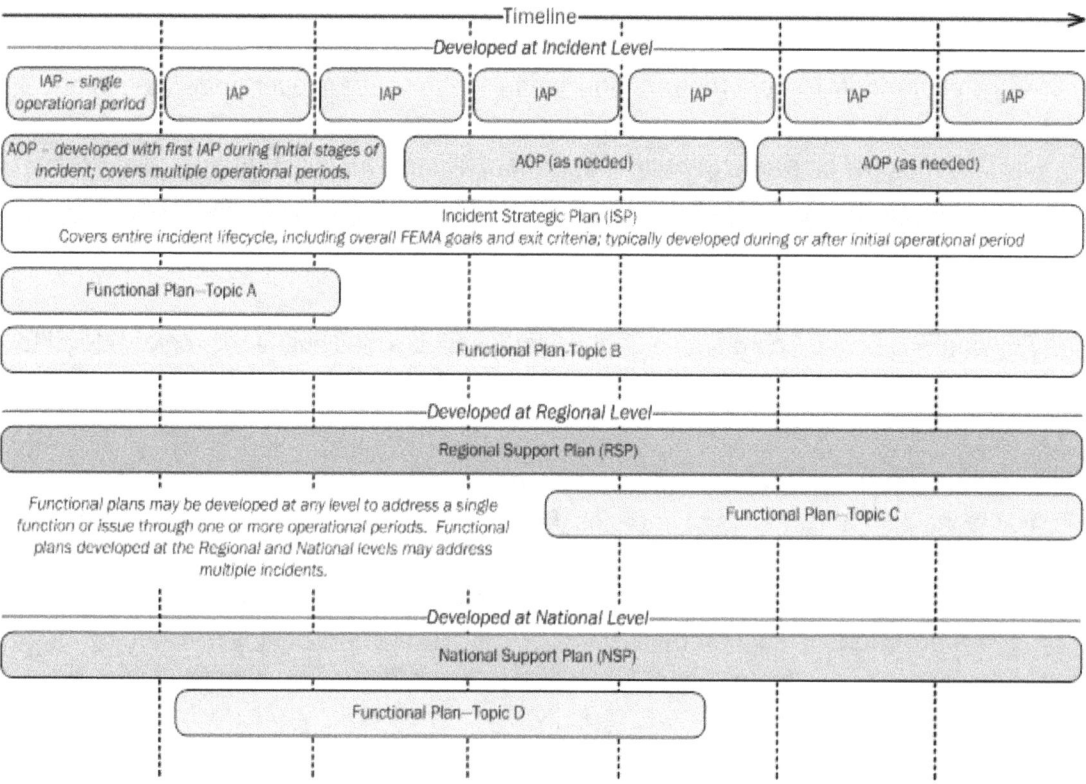

Figure 2. Incident plans shown in the context of an incident timeline

Concept 17: There Is Only One Incident Action Plan (IAP) for Each Incident, and the IAP Is Developed Only at the Incident Level

FEMA response and recovery operations are conducted in accordance with the NIMS. The principles of NIMS guide FEMA incident operations and planning. The ICS component of NIMS uses an iterative planning process called *incident action planning*. FEMA maintains a deliberate planning process that provides a conceptual basis for incident planning. FEMA incident management command and general staff use this process to produce a written IAP for each operational period.[3]

The IAP is a key element of incident planning and guides FEMA operations associated with the incident. It is developed under the direction of the UCG, which comprises senior leaders representing, at a minimum, Federal and State governments and may include senior leaders from tribal governments, local jurisdictions, and/or the private sector. Regardless of the membership, the purpose of the UCG is to establish and achieve shared objectives.

Regional and national support planning efforts reinforce the incident priorities and objectives but do not replace the IAP. The objectives outlined in the IAP cannot be changed at higher levels.

Concept 18: Effective Incident Planning Requires a Comprehensive System for Information Collection, Sharing, and Analysis That Includes All Echelons of an Incident

Information must flow up to senior leaders and back to incident managers to ensure that all levels of leadership have the knowledge they need to make informed decisions.

Information Management

Information management is performed to provide responders and planners with incident information that is tailored to meet the need for decision makers to have a common operating picture of the information management structure.

To be effective, planning must be based on accurate, timely information. Planning requires a system for information collection, analysis, and sharing among all levels; however, decision

---

[3] "Operational Period: The time scheduled for executing a given set of operation actions, as specified in the Incident Action Plan. Operational periods can be of various lengths, although usually they last 12 to 24 hours." NIMS, December 2008, p. 144.

makers must assume additional risk in a disaster environment when information is limited and, at times, inaccurate.

Collection is a continual and iterative process, with data integrated at every level. Collection ensures that decision makers at the incident, regional, and national levels are supplied with the data necessary to accurately understand the situation. Collection requirements are based on critical information requirements and essential elements of information (EEI). These pose—and hopefully answer—the questions that are vital to making the correct incident management decisions.

Critical information requirements are items of information regarding the situation and environment, which senior leaders need by a specified time to assist them in reaching decisions. Essential elements of information, derived from deliberate plans, are a comprehensive list of information requirements that are also needed to promote informed decision making. Essential elements of information are prioritized to answer the essential questions of the FCO or UCG needed at that time in the incident.

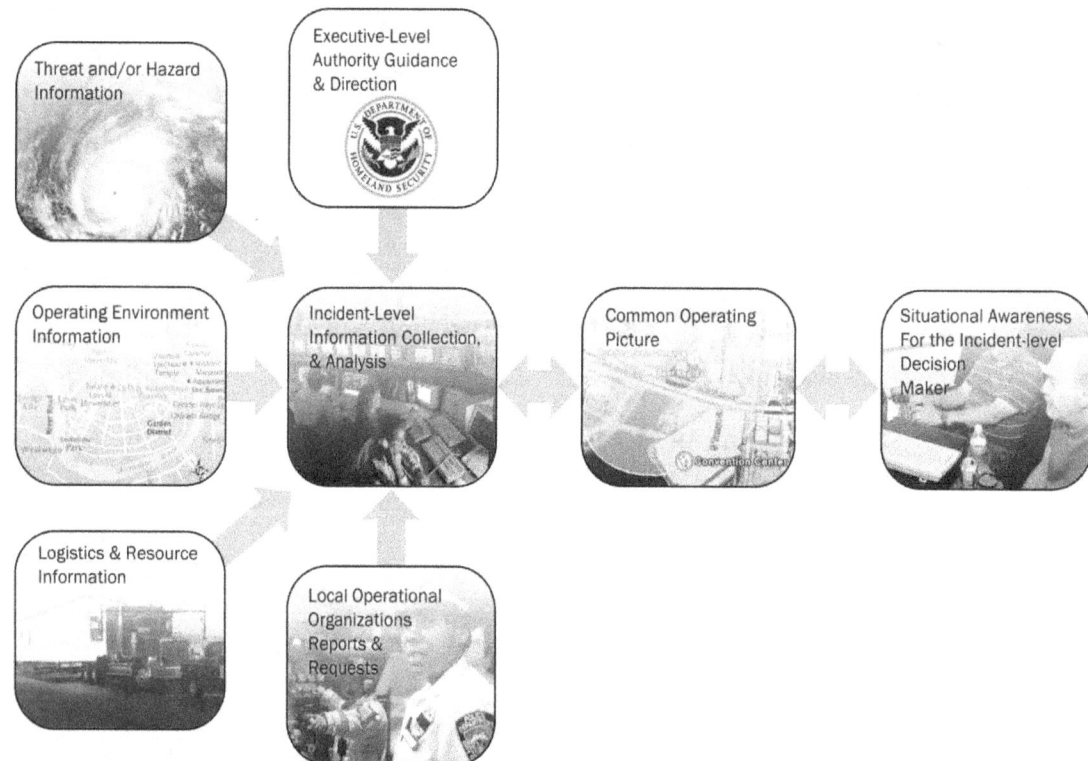

Figure 3: Relationship among collection, analysis, the common operating picture, and situational awareness

Analysis provides the UCG and other senior leaders with relevant information about the situation. Analysis verifies and validates raw data, when possible, then identifies relevant information for answering critical information requirements to help decision makers address pressing concerns. It is used to ensure that incident management and support activities are based on the most accurate and relevant information available. Analysis is also valuable in spotting emerging developments, such as rising shelter occupancy rates. The earlier these developments are detected, the greater the flexibility in resolving the issues.

Dissemination is information shared to assist decision makers in fulfilling their responsibilities. Shared situational awareness minimizes confusion, reduces duplication of effort, and provides a basis for effective and efficient resource management. For emergency managers to clearly understand the needs of the UCG, information must be shared in all directions so that a complete picture of pertinent information that may affect decisions and support elements is provided.

CONCEPT 19: DELIBERATE PLANNING IS THE FOUNDATION FOR INCIDENT PLANNING

Deliberate planning is the means by which leaders anticipate specific hazard or threat scenarios and envision desired outcomes, develop effective ways of achieving the desired outcome, and communicate decisions. A plan is an evolving instrument describing anticipated actions that will maximize opportunities and guide response operations. Since planning is an ongoing process, a plan is always an interim product based on information and understanding at the moment. As an interim product, a deliberative plan is always subject to revision.

Deliberate plans do not provide all the information needed to respond to an incident; however, such plans can be adapted to provide the best starting point for incident management. Deliberate plans that are well conceived and pertinent to an incident that occurs can actually provide the basis for IAPs for the initial operational periods, describing objectives, resource requirements, taskings, and priorities.

Good deliberate plans give incident managers an important head start on incident response. For no-notice incidents, the benefits of this head start may be measured in terms of actual lives saved.

CONCEPT 20: DELIBERATE PLANNING IS ONLY AS EFFECTIVE AS ITS ABILITY TO GUIDE ACTUAL OPERATIONS

Consistent use of a standardized and proven deliberate planning process and plan format facilitates planning and enhances the value of the plans produced.

There are many ways to produce deliberate plans. For FEMA planners, using a standard planning process to produce a plan in a format that is equally applicable and acceptable to State, local, and private-sector partners improves joint planning.

The value of a deliberate plan is determined by the accuracy of its risk or hazard analysis, the adequacy of the resources provided for in the plan, and the acceptability of the plan to those who must implement it.

The measure of a good deliberate plan is not whether execution in an actual incident transpires exactly as planned, but whether the plan facilitates effective organization, communication, and action in the face of unfolding events.

An effective deliberate planning process does the following:

- Engages all stakeholders

- Attempts to reduce the unknowns in the anticipated incident and acknowledges the impossibility of planning for every contingency and every aspect of the mission area

- Uses facts, including knowledge regarding people's likely behavior, the threat or hazard itself (gathered through modeling or disaster simulation), and required capabilities

- Focuses on developing general principles while maintaining flexibility for action and innovation

- Includes a period to train, exercise, and test the plan once it is developed

- Continuously incorporates new hazard information, best practices, and lessons learned

Chapter 6: Applying FEMA Incident Management and Support Doctrine

Key Roles and Responsibilities

The following section outlines the functions of key officials and structures in the conduct of FEMA incident management and support. This outline is not intended to document all the incident management and support activities but rather to describe the key roles and responsibilities—at the national, regional, and incident levels—of those who collaborate to achieve unity of effort.

National

At FEMA Headquarters, many organizational elements and individuals play key roles in incident support. The FEMA Administrator, the Director of Disaster Operations (DDO), the National Watch Center, and the National Response Coordination Staff (NRCS) have lead roles and responsibilities, described in the following section.

Figure 4. National organizational structure

FEMA Administrator

The FEMA Administrator is the principal advisor to the President,[4] the Secretary of Homeland Security, and the National Security Staff on all matters regarding emergency management.[5]

---

[4] Per the Robert T. Stafford Disaster Relief and Emergency Assistance Act, the President is responsible for declaring a disaster or emergency.

[5] See the Post-Katrina Emergency Management Reform Act, enacted as part of the FY 2007 DHS Appropriations Act, Public Law 109-295.

The Administrator has overall responsibility for FEMA's response and recovery operations. When FEMA is engaged in a specific incident or potential incident, the Administrator ensures optimal flow of information and coordination between FEMA and DHS Headquarters. The Administrator keeps the Secretary of Homeland Security informed regarding incident status, activities, and issues, and the Administrator resolves problems or issues that cannot be resolved at lower levels.

Director of Disaster Operations

The DDO is the senior FEMA official designated by the FEMA Administrator to coordinate and synchronize all Headquarters operational activities for credible threats during major disaster or emergency activations.

In dealing with a specific incident or potential incident, the DDO does the following:

- Ensures information flow and coordination among all FEMA operational levels— national, regional, and incident(s)

- Coordinates and synchronizes all Headquarters disaster response operations, programs, and related activities

- Provides appropriate incident support to the Regional Administrators (RAs) and Federal Coordinating Officers (FCOs)

- Directs deployment of national teams as needed

- Advises the FEMA Administrator on program and policy issues related to incident management and support and provides recommended courses of action

FEMA National Watch Center

The FEMA National Watch Center provides around-the-clock situational awareness for FEMA by doing the following:

- Supporting the collection and distribution of pre-incident information to the National Operations Center for the development of the national common operating picture

- Providing analysis of collected information and national situational awareness of potential, developing, or ongoing situations that may require a Federal response

National Response Coordination Staff

The National Response Coordination Center for FEMA disaster response is activated by the DDO in anticipation of, or in response to, an incident by activating the National Response Coordination Staff, which includes FEMA personnel, appropriate Emergency Support Function (ESF) representatives, and other personnel (including representatives of nongovernmental organizations [NGOs] and the private sector, when appropriate) to coordinate with the affected Region(s) and provide needed resources and policy guidance to support an incident.

The National Response Coordination Staff provides national emergency management coordination, conducts operational planning, deploys national resources, and collects and disseminates incident information as it builds and maintains national situational awareness. The National Response Coordination Staff does the following:

- Maintains situational awareness of specific potential threats or incidents
- Activates and deploys national teams, as the DDO, RA, or FCO directs
- Coordinates with the National Operations Center
- Coordinates support and situational reporting with the Regional Response Coordination Center
- Collects, validates, analyzes, and distributes incident information
- Deploys initial response resources and other disaster commodities when required
- Coordinates with the affected Region(s) to identify and report initial requirements for Federal assistance
- Develops National Support Plans to source and address identified resource shortfalls

Regional

The ten Regions are FEMA's first line of disaster response. For any given incident, FEMA disaster response begins and ends with the affected Region in the lead. The RA, the Regional Watch, and the Regional Response Coordination Center have central roles throughout the life cycle of an incident.

FEMA Regional Administrator

The FEMA RA is the primary FEMA representative to State governors, other Federal departments and agencies, and State, tribal, and local emergency management authorities during day-to-day operations.

When the Region is not actively engaged in an incident, the RA operates an around-the-clock watch and maintains an Incident Management Assistance Team (IMAT) capable of managing a Level II disaster.

After the President has declared a major disaster or emergency, the RAs have control of FEMA resources committed within their Regions. The RAs delegate directive authority for incident management and control of assigned Federal resources to the FCO when the FCO has established operational capability.[6]

---

[6] Operational capability: The attainment of the ability to employ required and effective response capabilities that are staffed by adequately trained, equipped, and supported responders.

For an anticipated or actual incident, the RA does the following:

- Activates and oversees the Regional Response Coordination Center staff
- Assists State authorities in conducting damage assessments
- Assist States with the major disaster or emergency declaration process
- Coordinates with the DDO on designating the disaster type (to ensure the request of resources and support)

When a Stafford Act emergency or major disaster has been declared, the RA does the following:

- Delegates Disaster Recovery Manager authority [7]
- Delegates control of regional Federal resources to the FCO when the FCO has established operational capability
- Provides oversight of incident management
- Provides guidance and direction to the FCO and ensures that incident objectives and priorities are appropriate and sufficient throughout the life cycle of an incident
- Ensures the proper transfer of authority when there is a change of FCO
- Reviews and approves the FCO's transition and demobilization plan
- Establishes requirements for transition of the FCO's control of assigned Federal resources to the RA

Regional Watch Center

Each FEMA region maintains an around-the-clock watch capability to make the RA and the RA's staff aware of potential, developing, or ongoing situations that may require Federal response. The Regional Watch Center collects and distributes information to the National Watch Center for development of national situational awareness. In several FEMA regions, the Mobile Emergency Response Support Operations Centers (MOC) provide this watch capability to the Regional Administrator.

Regional Response Coordination Staff

Each of FEMA's regional offices maintains a Regional Response Coordination Center. The RA stands up the center by activating the Regional Response Coordination Staff, which includes FEMA personnel, the appropriate ESF representatives, and other personnel (including representatives of NGOs and the private sector when appropriate) to provide needed

---

[7] 44 CFR 206.41.(b)

resources and policy guidance to support an incident and coordinate with the National Response Coordination Staff. The staff coordinates Federal and regional response efforts and maintains connectivity with State emergency operations centers, state fusion centers, and other Federal and State operations and coordination centers.[8]

Before the FCO assumes control of the Federal response, the Regional Response Coordination Staff will do the following:

- Establish and maintain the Regional Response Coordination Center, including ESF coordinators

- Contact the emergency operations center in the affected State(s) to identify capabilities and anticipate shortfalls to determine initial response requirements

- Implement processes for collecting, analyzing, and disseminating incident information to all appropriate parties

- Activate and deploy Federal assets

- Establish mobilization centers and staging areas, as needed

- Deploy appropriate Regional IMATs

- Request deployment of a national IMAT or additional IMATs from other Regions

Once the FCO has assumed control, the Regional Response Coordination Staff will do the following:

- Maintain situational awareness of the incident to support the RA's incident management oversight role, transitioning to the Regional Watch as soon as the situation allows

- Develop and implement Regional Incident Strategic Plans as needed to source and address identified resource shortfalls for complex or multiple incidents

Incident Level

FEMA's incident level refers to the level for which operational control of FEMA incident operations, including the Federal resources deployed to an incident and the establishment of

---

[8] Many states and larger cities have created State and local fusion centers to share information and intelligence within their jurisdictions as well as with the Federal government. The Department of Homeland Security, through the Office of Intelligence and Analysis, provides personnel with operational and intelligence skills to the fusion centers. This support is tailored to the unique needs of the locality and serves to do the following:
- Help the classified and unclassified information flow
- Provide expertise
- Coordinate with local law enforcement and other agencies
- Provide local awareness and access

a Unified Coordination Group (UCG), is delegated to an FCO or Federal Resource Coordinator. The extent of an incident is declared or determined by the principal authority, and the boundaries are specifically defined—such as a given State (or States), enumerated counties, a city, or any combination of jurisdictions involved.

Federal Coordinating Officer

The FCO coordinates Federal support in the response to and recovery from emergencies and major disasters declared under the Stafford Act. The RA delegates control of FEMA incident operations—including the Federal resources deployed to the incident—and Disaster Recovery Manager authority to the FCO, once the FCO establishes operational capability. The FCO is appointed only for Stafford Act incidents and serves as the primary Federal representative to the State Coordinating Officer. For non-Stafford Act incidents, the Department of Homeland Security (DHS) may designate a Federal Resource Coordinator to perform essentially the same functions that the FCO performs but without the specific Stafford Act authorities. In these non-Stafford Act incidents, the Federal Resource Coordinator coordinates support through interagency agreements and memorandums of understanding; through senior Federal, State, local, and tribal officials; and with representatives of relevant private organizations and NGOs.

The FCO is the focal point of Federal coordination within the UCG, ensuring overall integration of Federal emergency management, resource allocation, and integration of Federal activities in support of, and in coordination with, State, tribal, and local government officials. The FCO does the following:

- Accepts the appointment from the FEMA Administrator to ensure that Federal assistance is provided in accordance with the declaration, applicable laws, and FEMA/State agreements[9]

- Accepts the delegation of Disaster Recovery Manager authority, control of regional Federal resources, and guidance from the RA

- Takes immediate action to reduce the threats to life, property, public health and safety, and the environment

- Ensures that a UCG is formed

- Identifies and establishes a Joint Field Office in coordination with the State Coordinating Officer

- Determines Federal assistance needs and arranges required support

- Establishes incident priorities and objectives in collaboration with other members of the UCG

---

[9] 44 Code of Federal Regulations (CFR), Emergency Management and Assistance, Part 206—Field Disaster Assistance; 44 CFR 206.41, Appointment of Disaster Officials, Federal Coordinating Officer (current as of 2009).

- Assigns tasks and responsibilities to other Federal departments and/or agencies

- Ensures that the Federal incident management and support structure is appropriate to meet the needs of the incident and is structured on the principles of the National Incident Management System (NIMS) and the Incident Command System (ICS)

- Ensures that incident information is complete, validated, analyzed, and disseminated appropriately

- Ensures that adequate safety measures are in place and that safety practices are observed

- Resolves issues at the incident level and raises issues to the Region and/or FEMA Headquarters level for resolution when required

- Ensures that an efficient and orderly transfer of authority is conducted when transferring command to another FCO

- Develops, coordinates, and approves the Incident Transition or Demobilization Plan

- Coordinates release priorities for assigned resources with the RA

FEMA's Incident Command and Management Organization

Command and General Staff

The FCO's command and management organization is defined in ICS as the command and general staff, which are responsible for overall management of FEMA's incident operations. The command and general staff direct FEMA's operations from the Joint Field Office, which is generally located at or near the incident site.

Command Staff

The Command Staff is responsible for advising the FCO and is assigned responsibility for key activities, including external affairs, safety, and liaison. A Chief of Staff is often included, as required by incident circumstances.

- **External affairs** is a relatively large function managing the interface with the public, the media, and/or other agencies with incident-related information requirements

- **Safety** monitors incident operations and advises the FCO on matters relating to safety

- **Liaison** functions as the point of contact for representatives of assigned and cooperating organizations to provide input on their agency's policies, resources availability, and other incident-related matters

- The **Chief of Staff** is responsible for coordinating and facilitating the functioning of the Command Staff

The General Staff is responsible for the functional aspects of the incident command structure. The sections of the General Staff are responsible for the operations, planning, logistics, and finance and administration functions.

- The **Operations Section** manages the operations that coordinate the delivery of Federal assistance programs and services, including lifesaving assistance (urban search and rescue, medical, evacuations support, etc.), life-sustaining assistance (shelter, water, food, etc.), individual assistance, public assistance, hazard mitigation assistance, environmental planning and historic preservation compliance, disaster emergency communication, staging of resources, community recovery, and other Federal support to supplement State and local government efforts.

- The **Planning Section** collects, analyzes, validates, and disseminates incident information to the UCG, incident personnel, and regional and national coordination centers. This section facilitates and develops all incident plans. It is also responsible for the check-in and status of all assigned resources and for maintaining accurate, timely incident files.

- The **Logistics Section** provides facilities, services, and material in support of the incident. It is responsible for transportation, supplies, food, communications and information technology, and medical services. It is also responsible for establishing a Single Point Order Tracking system to centrally manage and track resource orders for disaster supplies, equipment, services, personnel, and teams throughout FEMA. Resource ordering can occur at multiple echelons simultaneously.

- The **Finance/Administration Section** manages and supervises all financial, administrative, and cost analysis. This section is also responsible for funds control, document control, personnel actions, personnel time, travel voucher preparation, acquisitions, and administering compensations and claims.

Emergency Support Functions

FEMA coordinates incident response support from across the Federal government by activating, as needed, one or more of the 15 ESF teams. Federal ESFs are the primary mechanism for grouping Federal functions most frequently used in emergency management. ESFs provide the structure for organizing, planning, and deploying Federal interagency support to domestic disasters and emergencies. Each ESF is composed of one or more primary agencies and supporting agencies and organizations.

ESF resources may be assigned to the command and general staff, as well as to the Regional Response Coordination Center and the National Response Coordination Center. While the primary agency representatives of given ESFs are typically assigned to specific sections for management purposes, ESF resources may be assigned anywhere and to multiple locations, as required, within incident management and support structures.

CONCLUSION

The information provided in the document applies to all types of FEMA incidents—from small floods that affect only two counties to catastrophes that devastate thousands of people in many states and multiple FEMA Regions. While the doctrine provides authoritative guidance that is specific and quite detailed in some cases, it is intended to be applied by FEMA professionals exercising good judgment and applying the expertise they have gained through experience and training.

Generally speaking, the exact applicability of the standard guidance will decrease as the disaster type increases. Guidance that applies fully and quite literally for a Type III incident may provide a general doctrinal context for dealing with a Type I incident.

The guidance is not intended to preclude well-considered innovation or the exceptions that FEMA leaders must make to properly perform their demanding jobs—under conditions that are rapidly changing and that may involve life-or-death decisions.

www.ingramcontent.com/pod-product-compliance
Lightning Source LLC
Chambersburg PA
CBHW080543290526
45790CB00006B/2528